WESLEYAN THEOLOGICAL PERSPECTIVES

THE CHURCH
JESUS BUILDS

S0-AGV-387

Compliments of...

wesleyan publishing house

P.O. Box 50434
Indianapolis, IN 46250-0434

Call: 800.493.7539 • Fax: 800.788.3535
E-mail: wph@wesleyan.org • Online: www.wesleyan.org/wph

Please send copies of any review or mention.

WESLEYAN THEOLOGICAL PERSPECTIVES

THE CHURCH JESUS BUILDS

*A Dialogue on the Church
in the 21st Century*

Edited by Joseph Coleson

wesleyan
publishing
house

Indianapolis, Indiana

Copyright © 2007 by Wesleyan Publishing House
Published by Wesleyan Publishing House
Indianapolis, Indiana 46250
Printed in the United States of America

ISBN-13: 978-0-89827-349-6
ISBN-10: 0-89827-349-8

To the honor and memory of all who have loved
and served the church, this volume
is affectionately dedicated

CONTENTS

FOREWORD

My childhood was churchless, with four brief exceptions. The first was a month of Sunday school classes in the basement of a small Nazarene church in southern Idaho. I was six years old when Mrs. Trammel, a family friend, got my parents' permission to take my younger sister, two younger brothers, and me to church with her on Sunday mornings.

My next experience, which took place two or three years later, was a six-week introduction to Methodism. My adoptive father suffered a heart attack at age thirty-three. As soon as he was well enough, my folks thought we should do something to thank God for making him better. We all dutifully filed into a pew, mom at one end, the four of us children in the middle, and dad blocking the escape route. I don't recall much about Methodists, aside from wondering why the man who did most of the talking during the service wore a black dress and colored scarf.

A couple of years later, two laymen from the Church of Christ visited our home. I watched as they showed my parents a flip-chart presentation of the plan of salvation at our dining room table. Mom and Dad were impressed. So, for the next two Sundays, they let strangers stop at our house and take my siblings and me across town to church. I had my first communion there. The bread was okay, but I passed up the little cups when the man who brought us to church told me what was in them and I told him I didn't really care much for grape juice.

My fourth childhood religious encounter came when I was twelve — a seven-night prophecy conference at my birth father's Seventh Day

Adventist church. I earned a white, leatherette, King James Version Bible by attending the services and underlining the verses that the evangelist talked about with red and blue colored pencils. I don't recall what each color symbolized, but I think it was important for the proper outcome of the end times to get them right.

My ecumenical years bore little fruit. While I'm sure they contributed to an awareness of God's existence, He had little to do with my life as far as I knew. By the time I turned thirteen, my mother and adoptive father had divorced and she was married for a fourth time. We moved to a little logging town in north-central Idaho. Soon, another divorce disrupted our family. Mom decided to go back to live with my grandparents, but I wanted to finish my sophomore year at my current high school. So at age fifteen, I told my mother I wanted to live on my own. I moved out, and she drove away.

Then something wonderful happened: A Wesleyan pastor and his wife heard about my situation and invited me to live with them. Through their kindness, the persistent invitations of two high school friends, a church youth group that welcomed me, and the intercession of a group of believers who met one night each week to pray for people like me who were not yet Christians, I came face-to-face with the realization of how much I needed the God in whom I barely believed. Convicted of my sins, convinced of righteousness, and longing to know Jesus Christ for real, I knelt in the pastor's study late one evening and poured out a prayer for Him to forgive my sins and come into my life. Faith was born. Angels sang! I became a new creation in Christ.

Over the next two years, I was discipled by godly teachers and friends; baptized into the family of God; reunited with my family; equipped to share my faith with others; and encouraged to obey God's call to vocational ministry by a new pastor, who modeled the fervent holiness he preached. My life was changed forever by coming into contact with this little outpost of the kingdom of God located in an out-of-the-way mountain village.

My story is not unique. It has been told millions of times before, and—Please, Lord!—it will be retold millions of times again in countless other places until Jesus returns. It is the story of people coming together to help other people come to God. It is the story of the world's greatest transformational movement—a movement called the Church.

More specifically, it is the story of the Church Jesus is building. This beautiful Church is a sight to behold. It is the body of Christ— the mystical flesh through which the living God reaches out to a dying world. It is an unfinished masterpiece on which the Lord continues to work. Although not yet all that it will be, the Church is already full of the optimism of grace, confidently offering hope, healing, and full salvation to lost and broken people.

The Church Jesus builds is a missional community that embraces searchers and saints simultaneously, calling them to holiness and shaping them into the image of Christ's likeness. It is the mouthpiece of God, speaking clearly for Him in Word and sacrament, instruction and inspiration, worship and good deeds. It teaches the truth even when people cannot stand the truth. It exudes compassion that makes others feel they are being loved by God himself. The Church Jesus builds exists to multiply wholehearted followers of Christ. It has a billion faces, but its unity is not threatened by its diversity.

There are not many other books on ecclesiology like this one. Each essay in these refreshing pages views the Church through Wesleyan eyes. The insights here will strengthen your delight in partnering with God in the greatest work in the world. Prepare yourself to fall more deeply in love with the Bridegroom as you catch new glimpses of His Bride.

—Dr. Jerry Pence, General Superintendent, The Wesleyan Church

EDITOR'S PREFACE

This is the second volume in the *Wesleyan Theological Perspectives* series. The first volume, *Passion, Power, and Purpose: Essays on the Art of Contemporary Preaching*, was published in June of 2006. These volumes, and those to follow in the series, are one realization of a vision of Wesleyan scholars—including, but not limited to, those in the religion and philosophy divisions of our various church-related institutions—to contribute to the fulfillment of Jesus' command to make disciples throughout the world, and to assist our ministerial brothers and sisters in doing so. These volumes are intended primarily for pastors and other ministers, and for those preparing for vocational ministry, especially in The Wesleyan Church and our sister denominations and groups within the Wesleyan/Holiness theological tradition.

It is fitting to express our thanks from the very beginning to the presidents of the educational institutions of The Wesleyan Church, who together comprise the Wesleyan Education Council. They immediately and warmly embraced the entire project, of which this series is a part, and allocated significant funding to make it happen. The project as a whole is called "Jerusalem 50," a reminder that the Church began in Jerusalem on the Day of Pentecost, came to the conclusion that God welcomes Gentiles into the Church at the Jerusalem Council around A.D. 50, and anticipates the fullness of the Eschaton in Jesus' *parousia*, and the unveiling of the New Jerusalem.

The choice of volume topics for the series has been something of an *ad hoc* process. However, *ad hoc* does not mean *haphazard*. *Passion, Power, and Purpose* came first because we knew good pastors and other preachers are always looking for help and inspiration to make their preaching even better. We also knew that our universities, North American Bible College, and Wesleyan-approved seminaries have Wesleyan professors with both the preaching and the academic learning and experience to make a worthwhile contribution. We knew if we did it right, that volume would get the series off to a good start.

We decided this volume on ecclesiology should be next for many reasons, including the realization that it is possible for a person to attend a Wesleyan church for weeks or months without learning what bonds Wesleyans with other Christians, and what distinguishes us from the other major traditions within the broader Christian faith. As students of, for, and in the church, we agreed that the church must be both incarnational and eschatological, if it is to be both biblical and Wesleyan. This recognition gave us two lenses through which to consider other important characteristics of the Church in all its manifestations— local and denominational, national and international, attractional and missional, etc.

The "academic" contributors to this volume have extensive experience in the local church, as members, as volunteer workers, and in pastoral and other paid positions. We realized, however, that a volume on ecclesiology would be vastly better for also including contributions from persons currently working full time in local church settings. If you care to know which contributors are which, you may learn from "About the Authors" in the back of the volume. When you have finished reading the book, we think you'll agree both groups were necessary to make this volume what it is.

We know, of course, that this small volume cannot address all pertinent issues, cannot be the final word on ecclesiology. We offer it to you, our brothers and sisters—in The Wesleyan Church and beyond—only in the fond hope that it will be the beginning of your falling in love all over again with the Church for which Christ died, and for which He shall return again in glory.

Other volumes in the series are projected to appear on approximately a yearly schedule. It is the hope and prayer of all who have contributed to these first two volumes that their usefulness and inspiration will engender in you, our readers and co-laborers in the gospel, an agreeable anticipation of future volumes.

INTRODUCTION

Joseph Coleson

A few years ago, a group of Wesleyans came by plane to our quadrennial General Conference. On the way into town from the airport, the shuttle driver asked the group why they had come to his city. When they said they were there for the denominational General Conference, he asked, "What church are you with?" They responded, "The Wesleyan Church." He replied, "Never heard of it." Then he said he himself was a churchgoer. When they asked what church he attended, he replied with the name of a local Wesleyan church! To be fair to that local church, its pastor, and the man himself, he and his family had only just begun attending.

This anecdote does, however, illustrate some of the issues surrounding the topic of this volume, namely ecclesiology and the importance of giving it serious reflection. Ecclesiology is the study of the Church—its essence; its relationships with God, its members, and the world; its calling and commission; its God-ordained future.

A CONVERSATION ABOUT THE CHURCH

As the editorial committee responsible for this series met to plan this volume, we thought a conversation among the contributors, after they had written their own chapters, could prove to be a valuable addition to the book. We didn't know; such conversations included in books are rare. We thought it worthwhile to try, however, so most of the contributors gathered for a conversation on a Thursday afternoon and a Friday morning. I was tasked with writing up a summary of that conversation. We, the contributors, found it to be an encouraging, stimulating, and valuable time. We hope this summary of the main points of our conversation will give you, the reader, an idea of where we are coming from and what we hope to say as Wesleyans who love the Church and minister in, to, and for her in a variety of ways.

One contributor opened our conversation by saying, "How preachable this is!" He went on to say he had taken notes on possible sermon passages, topics, points, and even illustrations. I have known this pastor for years. He did not say this to score points with the rest of us; it is his usual way. He recognizes, as do we all, the primacy of the preaching moment in the weekly life of the church. God can and does speak to God's people in many ways, but the primary worship service still is the most widely recognized occasion. This pastor, and all effective pastors, are on the lookout continually for "grist for the sermon mill," if you will, and pick it up wherever they find it. The Church Jesus builds is a worshiping/preaching/teaching/learning church; the pastor is the leader in that.

The theological term for the doctrines and the study of the Holy Spirit within the Trinity, and the Spirit's roles in leading and empowering Christ's body, the Church, is *pneumatology*. Our conversation turned to the fact that Wesleyanism is both incarnational and pneumatological. We mean, first of all, that Jesus builds the Church, intentionally, as His continuing Incarnation in the world. A well-known New Testament metaphor, of course, is that the Church is the body of Christ; that's what *incarnational* means. What Jesus was in the flesh while on this earth, the Church continues to be. What Jesus did while in the flesh on this earth, the Church continues to do, if she wholly and truly is the Church.

At the same time, Wesleyans, since John and Charles themselves, have understood that the Spirit working in and through the Church is the Spirit of Christ, the Third Person of the Trinity, sent by the Father and the Son for the Church's instruction, guidance, and empowerment. The Church cannot *be* the body of Christ, unless *indwelt* by the Spirit of Christ. The Church cannot *do* what the body of Christ is to do, unless *empowered* by the Spirit of Christ. In both their social reform and their revivalist histories, The Wesleyan Church and her sister denominations have recognized this and have sought the Spirit's indwelling and empowerment.

We noted that the various emphases of this volume, taken together, showcase the vastness of the Church, when many times we tend to focus on one aspect only, missing its totality and thus its God-gifted grandeur. We hope, if you read the book straight through within a reasonably concentrated time, you also will notice this and be renewed and encouraged in your love for God and God's Church.

We discussed the disconnection between our stated emphasis on the primacy of Scripture in guiding us as Wesleyan/Holiness folk, and our actual use—or lack thereof—of Scripture when it would seem natural to consult or appeal to it for guidance. The Wesleyan Church needs to retain and return to its emphasis on Scripture as the written Word, in its character and function as the first revealer of the Son, the Incarnate Word.

Some helpful questions on this point emerged: Have we become so pragmatic and experiential that we've lost the voice of biblical scholarship and understanding in our decision-making and in our practice? Has the role of the pastor shifted so much from "preacher" to "leader" that we no longer invest time, care, and prayer in serious exegesis and exposition? Can "leadership" really be *pastoral* leadership if it does not include the commitment of the pastor/leader, "I am a proclaimer of the Word of God to you"? Has our culture, including our church culture, become so much a therapeutic culture that we have lost the exegetical emphasis in our ministerial vocation? Has the loss of respect for biblical authority in the broader culture and its replacement by other sources of authority deflected the Church from its appropriate focus on Scripture, rightly understood as a continuing and primary source of authority for the Church?

Part of the reason for this apparent decline in our serious approach to the Bible in the church lies at the point of the greatest tension most preachers experience, in the crafting of the sermon. Most of us do not experience inordinate difficulty in discerning the major points of most biblical texts. But what comes next in the sermon?

One of the group, a long-time pastor, put it this way: "The pastor must identify clearly the major points of the text, then ask, 'How do the main biblical points become the main points of the message?' That's where the breakdown is for many pastors, and is one of the hardest things to connect to the congregation. The authority is lost there. The material preached may be compelling for people to hear, but it really has nothing to do with the authority of the text. But when you have the authority of the Word and put it in the context of the experiential, you have something very dynamic."

I must be content to record but one more comment that I think accurately describes the attitude of us all toward God's Church: "As ministers, we are caretakers; it's not *our* church. It's easy, in every-day 'church work,' to get used to it, then to miss the reverence of the whole. But how amazing [it is], how privileged we are to be a part of this!"

WHAT YOU'LL FIND IN THIS BOOK

In the conceptualization of this volume, we took the incarnational and the eschatological nature of the Church as central to a Wesleyan understanding of the Church. We did this because Wesleyanism views these as central to the biblical understanding of the Church, giving meaning, clarity, perspective, and depth to everything else we mean when we say, and when we speak of, "the Church."

Thus, chapter one is a survey of what it means for the Church to be incarnational, both locally and globally. In our conversation, the author of this chapter said, "I'm trying to underscore the connection between Christology and ecclesiology."

Chapter two is intended to set forth a biblical understanding of eschatology. That is, eschatology is not concerned only, or even primarily, with "the end times." Rather, the Scripture's own eschatological emphasis is on God's action, from the beginning, in redeeming humankind, and the rest of God's earthly creation, through Jesus' Incarnation, atoning death, and resurrection. The Church lives in the "already, but not yet," between the inauguration of the Kingdom in the Church, and our Bridegroom and King's return.

As their titles indicate, each of the subsequent chapters highlights one emphasis in the nature or the character of the Church. We do not imagine Wesleyans have a corner on these emphases, or that this book will have the final word on any of them. Rather, we offer our work as a contribution to the ongoing conversation about these important aspects of ecclesiology in the Wesleyan/Holiness tradition.

AN ILLUSTRATIVE REPORT

The following account was related during our contributors' conversation; it illustrates what we think God raised up the Church to be. The experience of this particular pastor and this local church (told here with permission) may be extraordinary for our day, but the point of including it is that we think it should not be so very extraordinary, after all. The details will differ from church to church, but the Spirit who directs and blesses Fountain City Wesleyan Church waits to bless all of God's people, wherever we gather in Jesus' name. The question is, will we let Him?

The Reverend Mr. David Anderson has been pastor of Fountain City Wesleyan Church in Indiana since graduating from seminary in

1984. In 1989, Fountain City was a fellowship of about ninety people who were concerned about personal piety and shared a burden for reaching their community.

That year, Pastor Dave had a vision from the Lord, literally, while fasting and spending a day alone with God. He is not accustomed to being visited with visions, but this one became a driving impetus for his ministry and for the church. In this vision, Dave saw many young children whose parents needed help giving them guidance. He saw teens walking the corridor of a school, then saw those same teens ten years later, their lives broken by wrong choices. Finally, he saw a large church building on a specific property a few miles away along a highway, at a location he recognized. Then a voice he understood as God's voice spoke, "Are you willing to be the one?" He knew the church had to say, "Yes." He knew, too, this would happen only through drastic change and by faith.

At first, Pastor Dave spoke of the vision only to his wife; she also thought it must be from God. They continued to pray and work and seek the Lord, but did not feel led to share the vision with the church until some months later. The church embraced the vision, though he did not at that time reveal the details about the location.

In 1990, the church began holding two services. Inexplicably, people began to join their small fellowship. A godly woman in the church, Mary McQuisten, independently felt led to offer acreage from her farm to the church, a further confirmation of the location given to Pastor Dave in his vision. In 1992, the church moved worship services to the cafeteria/auditorium at the high school on the highway. In 1994, they launched a capital campaign, and the next year borrowed a million dollars and started construction on a new building.

This did not happen without opposition from the Enemy. At a critical juncture, several key members of the church experienced oppression and even tragedy in various forms. But the church remained true to the vision. Today, after a second round of building, a large and growing church has its premises on the location shown to Pastor Dave in his vision. More than nine hundred people regularly worship and minister in the Fountain City Wesleyan Church fellowship.

Recently, Pastor Dave learned God gave a similar vision to a superintendent of another denomination in 1988, the year before his own vision. The local churches challenged by that superintendent to begin ministry at that location did not respond, so God found someone else, someone willing to see, to believe, and to act in faith.

No one else's experience will be quite the same as that at Fountain City. But God, who redeemed in Jesus all who will respond, who birthed the Church at Pentecost in the anointing of the Holy Spirit, who preserves and prospers the Church down the ages by that same Spirit, will bring us at last to himself, a glorious Church, without spot or wrinkle. What an amazing privilege, indeed, to be a part of God's Church!

THE CHURCH
JESUS BUILDS IS

The Church Jesus Builds Is

INCARNATIONAL

❖

J. Michael Walters

*And so you became a model to all the believers in Macedonia and Achaia.
The Lord's message rang out from you not only in Macedonia and
Achaia—your faith in God has become known everywhere.*

—1 Thessalonians 1:7–8

*How is it possible that the gospel should be credible, that people should
come to believe that the power which has the last word in human affairs is
represented by a man hanging on a cross? I am suggesting that the only
answer, the only hermeneutic of the gospel, is a congregation of men and
women who believe it and live by it . . . . [E]vangelistic campaigns, distri-
butions of Bibles and Christian literature, conferences, even books such as
this one . . . all are secondary, and . . . have power to accomplish their
purpose only as they are rooted in and lead back to a believing community. Jesus . . . did not write a book but formed a community.*

—Leslie Newbigin, *The Gospel in a Pluralistic Society*

I n the hamlets of East London, a little more than a kilometer from
the Tower itself, sits an imposing building known as Christchurch
Spitalfields. It was designed by the renowned architect Nicholas
Hawksmoor, and consecrated as a church in July 1729. Like many
old buildings, it fell into disrepair but was restored when funds were
secured through, of all avenues, something called the "Heritage
Lottery Fund." Today, Christchurch is again an imposing and beautiful
structure, but its primary significance these days is not owing to its

place as a British landmark but to its role in the kingdom of God. It is a poignant example of an incarnational church. In Newbigin's words, it is a "hermeneutic of the gospel," a visible means by which people can come to understand what *good news* means.

The Anglican rector (pastor) of Christchurch is a chap in his late thirties, by the name of Andrew Ryder. I was privileged to meet Andy a few months ago. After showing us the building, he offered to show his parish to me and two of my colleagues.

Spitalfields would not be high on the list for prospective church planters. It is a seedy, run-down, economically-challenged neighborhood, typical of East London. Unemployment and crime are high and most of the inhabitants struggle to make ends meet. Streetwalkers are evident. In fact, right across the street from the church building stands the infamous Ten Bells Tavern, Jack the Ripper's preferred haunt for selecting his victims. The tavern still operates, and the neighborhood clientele represents essentially the same moral outlook. As we walked along, Andy told us his church has a ministry to the sex workers on the street, offering them a place of sanctuary and basic hospitality, a place where they can be treated as something other than a commodity. He pointed to a part of the church's property that was being turned into a place to meet with at-risk youth of the area.

Just down the block from Christchurch stands one of the largest mosques in England. The neighborhood around this church has become the largest settlement of Bangladeshi people anywhere outside their home country, making Islam the predominant religious choice of the parish.

As we walked through the neighborhood, Andy seemed completely unfazed by the monumental barriers he faces in pastoring a church in such a location. Rather, he seemed genuinely energized by the prospect of finding ways to "be the church" in such a place. Perhaps the most obvious example of that conviction is the school

Christchurch sponsors. Its student population is predominantly neighborhood Muslim children, whose parents would deeply resent overt efforts by the church to convert them, to say nothing of how British law would interpret such actions. Given the inherent limitations of what they can do evangelistically with these children, I asked Andy why they were willing to commit such time and resources to the school. His answer was stunningly simple, "Because these children need to be educated."

From what I could gather, the Sunday crowd at Christchurch would not be impressive by any American church's standards. Nevertheless, I have seldom seen a church as committed to incarnating the values of the kingdom of God in their neighborhood, as this small Anglican parish is.

The story of Christchurch Spitalfields is important because it underscores the truth that the Church Jesus builds is first and foremost incarnational. The word *incarnation* means, literally, "in the flesh." The Church is intended to be a tangible, visible, "fleshly" imitation of Jesus himself. That's why Paul employed the term *body of Christ* to describe the Church. The concept of incarnation is fundamental not only to understanding the nature of the Church, but also to grasping the Church's mission and providing a means of evaluating its methods and strategies.

INCARNATION AS AN ECCLESIOLOGICAL KEY

"What's the most important word in the Bible for the Church?" is one of those teaching questions professors like to employ to set up discussion. Whenever I use this with either students or pastors, the results are predictable. Words like *love*, *grace*, and *hope* are quickly mentioned. But I have in mind another word, often overlooked when we read Scripture. The word is *as*. I have come to think that this little word is the single most important word for the Church to grasp in terms of understanding its nature in the world, and its mission. In the twentieth chapter of John's gospel, we find the disciples, on that first Easter Sunday, huddled together in fear behind closed doors. A church with its doors locked! Hardly an encouraging sight. Into that room, heavy with despair, came the resurrected Jesus, proceeding to commission His disciples. At the center of this commissioning are the breathtakingly awesome words, "*As* the Father has sent me, even so I send you" (John 20:21, RSV, emphasis added). In short, the Church's mission in the world is intended to be something of a continuation of Jesus' own Incarnation.

If we truly grasp the import of Jesus' words here, then we realize to call the Church "incarnational" is repetitious. Any congregation that claims to be a church but does not visibly model the person and mission of Jesus, engages in deception. By its very nature, the Church exists to embody what Jesus embodied in His own Incarnation.

Moreover, Jesus' Incarnation is a continuation, albeit unique in many ways, of what the Father has willed from the beginning of salvation history. From the outset of God's redemptive acts on behalf of humankind, the principle of incarnation was central. Abraham and his family, who would become the origins of Israel, were to be a visible, bodily example of what it meant to worship Yahweh. The people of Israel, as God's covenant people, were to live so clearly in harmony with the covenant that all the peoples of the earth would come to know that Yahweh is, indeed, God. In divine wisdom, God never left the human family, desperately in need of salvation, to guess what it entailed; He always gave us tangible models to observe and emulate. Despite ancient Israel's repeated failures in carrying out its mandated mission, Israel's history laid the groundwork for the Incarnation of Jesus and its subsequent and ongoing importance for the life of the Church.

A popular way of getting at this essence of incarnation is seen in the use of the phrase, "the scandal of particularity," which suggests that Jesus' Incarnation sweeps away all of our attempts to generalize God and the spiritual life. In Jesus, we have a clear picture of what it looks like to live in the reality of the kingdom of God come to this earth. It follows that when Jesus told those first disciples He was sending them into the world *as* the Father had sent Him into the world, His life and ministry became the very foundation of the Church.

When we think of Jesus' Incarnation, we are dealing with what C. S. Lewis termed "the grand miracle, the miracle by which all other miracles are made possible."[1] This idea is echoed by Australian theologians Michael Frost and Alan Hirsch: "The 'enfleshing' of God is so radical and total that it is the bedrock upon which rests all subsequent acts of God in His world." They go on to say, "A halfway house on the way to God would not do for a lost humanity, and so God had to come down to man, not halfway but the whole way."[2]

What does it say about God that He is willing to do this? What does it tell us about the nature of God when we see Him willingly putting on flesh to take the ultimate step in the redemption of His fallen creation? As Frost and Hirsch remind us, the Incarnation is about identification—God identifying completely and absolutely with fallen humanity. In this case, the medium is entirely the message. Most of what we really need to know about God is implicit in His Incarnation upon this earth. When Jesus submitted himself to the baptism of John, He symbolically "immersed" himself in the human condition; it was a microcosm of His entire ministry.

And now this same Jesus sends His Church into the world, just *as* the Father sent Him. The Church must see that all ecclesiology proceeds from Christology, what we affirm about Jesus. The Church is what it is because Jesus was and is who He is. Christ is the human image of God. Therefore, the Church, the body of Christ, is to emulate—to model to the world—what Jesus modeled about the Father. In *The Problem of Wineskins*, Howard Snyder says the Incarnation makes the study of God and the study of anthropology a Christological issue.[3] I would argue that it makes ecclesiology, our doctrine of the Church, an issue of Christology as well. John Wesley believed the vocation for which humans were created, and which is restored in salvation, is nothing less than to "live as the image of God in the world."[4] This is incarnational thinking at its best.

This imperative biblical and theological connection between Christ's Incarnation and the nature of the Church is what makes the visibility of the Church—its "located-ness," if you will—fundamental. Likely, every pastor has heard people who put off committing to a local church by claiming to belong to something they call "the invisible church." One might as well talk about permeable steel, or dry water. The very nature of the Church as the Incarnation, the continuing enfleshment of Christ, makes the notion of an invisible church impossible. In the same way that ice cream can't be hot and still be ice cream, the Church can't be invisible and still be the Church.

Incarnation is the necessary starting point of the process of *being* the Church. Apart from this identification with Christ—whatever else may be happening, no matter how impressive—we cannot claim it to be the work of the Church. To be sent *as* the Father sent Jesus must become the benchmark of any group of believers claiming to be a church, no matter where they exist in the world, and no matter under what circumstances they endeavor to live as God's people.

INCARNATION AS AN
ECCLESIOLOGICAL MODEL

A brief wander through any Christian bookstore today will yield dozens of titles aimed at helping people, clergy and laity alike, know "how to do church." I find this emphasis on *doing* church both amusing and unsettling. As I have argued above, ultimately the Church is about *being*. The teachings of Jesus and the entire New Testament underscore the necessity of keeping both *being* and *doing* in proper perspective. Indeed, one of the reasons Jesus irritated the religious thinkers of His own day was His readiness to emphasize being (the heart and mind) over doing (keeping the rules).

I have to confess to experiencing a certain amount of theological "heebie-jeebies" at the very notion of "doing" church. But for argument's sake, let's suppose all our intentions are honorable and we truly do want guidance on how the Church is supposed to conduct itself in the world. Where do we look? The answer, of course, is that we look at Jesus. If the Incarnation is the ecclesiological key for understanding the nature and character of the Church, then it is also the model for how the Church goes about its business in the world.

Recently, a colleague of mine picked me up at the airport, and as we drove along, he told me about a sermon he had preached in which he took some of Jesus' teachings and applied them to the modern Church. The sermon generated a few negative responses from some of the hearers who believed my colleague was being much too critical of the Church. At that point, my colleague said, "For most Christians, it would have been better for Jesus just to have been born and then to have died on the cross." I have found myself thinking about that statement a lot as I write this chapter. I believe my friend summarized all too well the mentality of many churches. We love Christmas, so we need to keep the birth narratives, Herod, and the angelic choir in the ecclesial repertoire. And obviously the Passion narrative, Good Friday and Easter, is central to the gospel, so it stays. But all this business about loving our enemies, giving our riches away, taking up *our* crosses, etc.—modern people just aren't about that. Of course, no one articulates it exactly like that, but I can't think of a better explanation for the state of the average American church these days, than to describe it as a wholesale failure to take Jesus seriously.

To be the ongoing Incarnation of Jesus means we never stray far from His own life and teachings. Remember, it's *"as* the Father sent me."* When Jesus commissioned His disciples in those words from Matthew 28, often hailed as the Great Commission, He specifically directed them to "go and make disciples of all nations, baptizing them in the name of the Father and of the Son and of the Holy Spirit, *and teaching them to obey everything that I have commanded you"* (Matt. 28:19–20, emphasis added). Jesus is the model. "Doing church" is nothing more than figuring out how to teach and apply the life and ministry of Jesus in our own day and time. Anything less is to betray our intended nature as an incarnational continuation of Jesus. Eugene Peterson writes, "Christ is the *way* as well as the truth and life. When we don't do it his way, we mess up the truth and we miss out on the life. We can't live a life more like Jesus by embracing a way of life less like Jesus."[5]

So, what was the *way* of Christ in the world? In what *way* was He sent by the Father? Clearly, Jesus' *way* in the world was noticeably different than the *way* of other religious figures of that day. When we give close attention to the life and teachings of Jesus, we find that He constantly took the values of the regnant culture and stood them on their proverbial heads. The poor were elevated, the outcasts were welcomed, the emphasis was on the small (for example, children), not the large and important. Jesus' way made Him stand out from the other wandering rabbis of the day, and attracted huge numbers of people who were eager to listen to what He proclaimed. In Jesus, we saw a totally revolutionary way of being in the world, the way of the Kingdom, and it is precisely *that* Kingdom that the Church is commanded to incarnate. Jesus literally came to model the Kingdom. He announced its arrival and cited His life, His miracles, and His teachings as evidence that such a Kingdom indeed had arrived on this earth. To incarnate Jesus means that the Church is to model Jesus' way as continuing evidence that the kingdom of God has come.

The Church, therefore, is an outpost of the Kingdom. Unfortunately, as my preaching friend learned, we have too commonly today a church grown adept at accommodating to and being shaped by the culture around it. Whenever the church stops keeping Jesus as the absolute central focus of its life and ministry, such accommodation is virtually inevitable. The church adopts values antithetical to the Kingdom it has been commissioned to expand.

Whenever and wherever we see racism, the subjugation of women, or the willingness of congregations to affirm by their silence the most un-Christian policies of governments, we know the church has gone astray. To be sure, Jesus may be proclaimed Head of the Church, but all the evidence points elsewhere. Jesus told His disciples they were to be in the world, but not of the world (John 17:14–16). Too many churches have turned Jesus' instructions around; we are often "of the world," but not "in the world." That is, we have readily adopted the world's ways, even while we have shut ourselves off from the kind of redemptive contact that epitomized the life of Jesus.

Using Jesus as our model would seem to be so obvious that it is unnecessary even to speak of this. But the evidence mounts that the Church has a tendency to move away from its "first love" (Rev. 2:4) and become representative of something besides the Kingdom that Jesus inaugurated in His Incarnation on earth. This has contributed to the tendency, as mentioned above, to speak of an "invisible church." Such talk makes it easy to rationalize the patently un-Christlike attitudes and behaviors that can be found so readily in the modern Church. As Brent Latham writes, "For too long, Christians have settled for the idea that the real Church can't be seen. It is invisible, known only to God but due to be revealed to the rest of us on the last day. Yet we should no more believe in such an invisible Church any more than the first disciples believed in an invisible Christ. The very purpose of the Church is to be a vision of who God is and what God is not."[6] This is why the Church must be incarnational—and unmistakably incarnational of *Jesus*!

Michael Budde shows the absolute absurdity of divorcing the Church's life and ways from Jesus, when he writes, "All of this is more than an idle exercise of theological speculation, for whatever we conclude God is or is not should have an important influence on what we think the church should or should not be. If God is merciful, the Church should not be vengeful; if God is not a white supremacist, neither should God's Church be a white supremacist institution."[7] The Church is a "vision of who God is and what God is not." That sounds terribly incarnational to me. If we take it seriously, we will have to rethink exactly how the Father "sent Jesus," so that we may, in turn, be the continuation of that original commission.

Obviously, this has profound implications for all matters of church life. The *way* of Jesus has something to say about how churches spend money, build buildings, and choose their locations. The imitation of Jesus has much to teach us about how we treat the unchurched people around us, how we involve ourselves in matters of local government, and how we might need to speak prophetically from time to time to those who "rule over us." Jesus' servant spirit has an invaluable role to play in enabling churches to grasp the essence of their mission on earth: to serve! His treatment of the marginalized can instruct us in how we should be relating to the "lepers" in our own social networks. It's worth remembering that when all is said and done, Jesus said His true followers would be recognized not by the size of their buildings or budgets, but by the depth of their love for one another. That is Jesus' way; it is also the way of any church that rightly claims His name.

Tim Costello, an Australian churchman, writes, "Ivan Illich was once asked what is the most revolutionary way to change society. Is it violent revolution or is it gradual reform? He gave a careful answer. Neither. If you want to change society, then you must tell an alternative story."[8] Christians have been given "an alternative story" to tell. Rather than the typical human story of power and coercion, we are to tell—no, we are to *live*—an alternative story of love, compassion, and peace. Jesus is how you "do" church.

INCARNATION AS A MISSIONAL STRATEGY

If Jesus' Incarnation is our ecclesiological key and our model for Church life, His Incarnation also must become the chart and compass of the Church's missional strategy. The word *missional* is used often these days in writings on the Church, and sometimes it takes on all the worst connotations of the kind of American pragmatism that is descriptive of an accommodationist, rather than of a faithful, obedient Church. Let's be clear—any talk of being missional in the Church *must* flow from our understanding of who Jesus was and what He came to this earth to do. As the body of Christ, the Church could not be otherwise. Thus, the Incarnation of Christ becomes the single most important factor in establishing the mission of the Church and thus the mission of any local manifestation of the Church.

From the beginning, the Incarnation underscores the basic character of the Church's mission: "As the Father has *sent* me, even so I am now *sending* you." Mobility is implied here. The Church's mission involves dynamism, movement, rather than the status quo. In light of this, it is ironic how easily the modern Church has adopted what Frost and Hirsch call an "attractional" rather than an incarnational ecclesiology. For example, most churches today operate with an understanding of evangelism that centers around mobilizing church members (or, in some cases, expecting the pastor to do it alone) to attract unbelievers into the church where they can experience God.[9] The basic evangelistic strategy is to organize "little patrols" to go into the world to rescue people and bring them back to the safety of church.

How odd that seems when compared with the life and ministry of Jesus! Jesus said He was "sent" by the Father. His life was a continuous series of journeys that brought Him into contact with people from all walks of life, people who had one thing in common: their need for God. In that light, a truly incarnational mode of evangelism would stress dynamic (changing) relationships and friendships. It would, in the words of Frost and Hirsch, continually seek ways to enhance and "flavor the host community's living social fabric rather than disaffirming it. It thus creates a medium of living relationships through which the gospel can travel. The missional-incarnational church starts with the basic theological understanding: God constantly comes to those who are the most unlikely."[10]

Where do we get such a theological understanding? From Jesus, of course. John wrote, "The Word became flesh and *dwelt* among us" (John 1:14, RSV). The Greek word for *dwelt* literally means "to tabernacle." Tabernacles are not permanent residences. The Israelites built a tabernacle, precisely because they were a people *on the move!* Jesus' Incarnation was intended to be mobile, not fixed.

By contrast, many of today's churches seem incapable of moving much of anything anywhere. We have succumbed to what I call a kind of "Zionist ecclesiology." At least one form of Zionism is the belief, held by radical Jews and by some Christians, that all of God's redemptive work for Israel must take place in certain geographical locales; unless the land of Israel is involved, God's hands are tied. A "Zionist ecclesiology" then is the understanding that all the work of God must take place *in* the Church, and mostly this means *in* the Church's buildings.

However, the history of Christian evangelism doesn't read that way at all. To assume we can simply retreat into our religious edifices to win our neighbors is both naive and a betrayal of the incarnational example of Jesus. Howard Snyder writes, "Church buildings attest to five facts about the Western Church: its immobility, inflexibility, lack of fellowship, pride, and class divisions. The gospel says, 'go,' but our buildings say, 'stay.' The gospel says, 'seek the lost,' but churches say, 'let the lost seek the church.'"[11] Because of our fixation on the church as buildings and programs, rather than on the church as a *people* committed to mobility, we've become champions at turning gifted people, who are meant to penetrate their worlds for Christ, into parking lot attendants, Sunday school attendance takers, or committee members—and we call it "ministry." Surely, that sounds hard, and perhaps it is. Legitimate reasons for church buildings and programs do exist, but the essential point is that in much of modern church life, we have come to emphasize something other than the incarnational character of the Church's mission.

A second major incarnational theme that ought to shape our mission is that of contextualization. We're not simply talking about Jesus; we're talking about Jesus of *Nazareth*! Contextualization is part of the Incarnation. Jesus was a Galilean Jew. He lived, worked, and ministered to the people of His day and time.

The modern Church can do no less. "Cultural exegesis," the ability truly to know and understand the traditions, mythology, and environmental character of one's own ministry locale, always should be prominent in the mind and the thinking of any church trying to ascertain or re-calibrate its mission. What is the nature of the relationship between a local church and the particular society it inhabits? How does a particular church incarnate the kingdom of God in its location? These are fundamental ecclesiological questions for our day, and no one from outside any given location is able to supply specific answers for that place. The life and teachings of Jesus, conscientiously applied to one's specific setting, is the only fail-proof methodology available to the Church today.

This is in keeping with the way Cardinal Avery Dulles has written of the Church as "sacrament."[12] A sacrament is a sign-act, or to use Augustine's phrase, "an outward and visible sign of an inward and spiritual grace."[13] Churches have to find ways to become visible signs of the Kingdom in their respective communities. The key to doing so is to pay proper attention to the Incarnation of Jesus of Nazareth. His life, His teachings, and His example provide the missional strategies for any church seeking to represent Him and God's kingdom faithfully on this earth.

CONCLUSION

By now, it should be clear I am contending that to describe the Church as incarnational is simply another way of calling the Church faithful. The relative absence of the term *church* in the teachings of Jesus convinces us that His major concern was to proclaim the coming of the kingdom of God. I have no doubt that the Church has been given this task. Furthermore, I have no doubt that the Church's ability to fulfill its purpose faithfully resides in its commitment to take Jesus seriously. As Brent Latham says, "Where the church fails to embody truly what God is, the world is left to believe in various not-gods."[14] Our world is filled with people believing in "various not-gods." The only antidote to this is a people whose lives and values bear an uncanny resemblance to the Jesus who long ago took on flesh and walked among us, showing us exactly who and what God looked like.

Let no one think for an instant this is easily done. That we see it so rarely today testifies to the difficulty of congregations truly incarnating Jesus in their lives and neighborhoods. But it can be done. As I walked the dingy streets of Spitalfields with Andy Ryder, I knew this kind of incarnational commitment is indeed the future of a church increasingly marginalized in society and considered irrelevant by many. And, lest we forget, it's not ultimately on us. It is ultimately on the Jesus who promised, "I will build my church, and the powers of death shall not prevail against it" (Matt. 16:18, RSV).

ACTION SUGGESTIONS

1. Do a "cultural exegesis" of your church's community, neighborhood, etc. What is the "story" of your place? In other words, what factors concerning your community have to be accounted for by the church? How would your church best serve your particular locale, not to entice people to come to your church, but simply to incarnate the Jesus who came, "not to be served, but to serve" (Matt. 20:28)?

2. Taking account of your church's property, buildings, etc., how could you best utilize what God has already given to incarnate His kingdom? How might you best employ your church property to become a more visible sign of the Kingdom's presence?

3. How can you take advantage of the ways the members of your church are "sent" into the world? Think of where they work, how they spend most of their time on the job, at home, etc. How could those people be unleashed to actually "be the church" in those parts of their lives that dominate most of their time and attention?

4. Which specific teachings of Jesus most complicate your present way of "doing church"? Why? If you were to take these teachings of Jesus seriously, what would change about the way you "do church"?

5. List some of the ways the Western Church has accommodated itself so much to the culture around it that it has lost its effectiveness as a witness to the kingdom of God. What needs to happen in your local church and in your denomination to remedy this problem?

FOR FURTHER READING

Clapp, Rodney. *A Peculiar People: The Church as Culture in a Post-Christian Society*. Downers Grove, Ill.: InterVarsity Press, 1996.

Clapp is certainly plugged into culture, yet he calls the Church to be its authentic self, rather than morphing into something unrecognizable in the name of "relevance."

Guder, Darrell L. *The Continuing Conversion of the Church*. Grand Rapids, Mich.: William B. Eerdmans Publishing Company, 2000.

Guder's synthesis of important ecclesiological writers like Leslie Newbigin, David Bosch, Jürgen Moltman, and Miroslav Volf is amazing. His call for the Church to recover its basic vocation as "witness" is compelling. Also, his take on the early Church and its commitment to mission could be revolutionary for pastors.

Hauerwas, Stanley. *A Community of Character*. Notre Dame: Notre Dame Press, 1981.

This is one of the first books I ever read on the Church, and I've never gotten over it; it is the genesis of all my ecclesiological interests. Hauerwas can be difficult to read, but the effort is definitely worth it.

Hauerwas, Stanley and **Willimon**, William H. *Resident Aliens: Life in the Christian Colony*. Nashville: Abingdon Press, 1989.

This book is cited in almost anything written on the subject of the present-day Church. It is prophetic, provocative, and engaging. The book is specifically aimed at the "mainline" church, but becomes increasingly relevant to the "evangelical" church, as it seems bent on making many of the same mistakes.

NOTES

1. C. S. Lewis, *Miracles* (New York: The Macmillan Company, 1978), 108.

2. Michael Frost and Alan Hirsch, *The Shaping of Things to Come* (Peabody, Mass.: Hendrickson Publishers, 2003), 35.

3. Howard Snyder, *The Problem of Wineskins* (Downers Grove, Ill.: InterVarsity Press, 1975), 88.

4. Theodore Runyon, *The New Creation: John Wesley's Theology Today* (Nashville: Abingdon Press, 1998), 12.

5. Eugene Peterson, *Christ Plays in Ten Thousand Places* (Grand Rapids, Mich.: William B. Eerdmans Publishing Company, 2005), 313.

6. Brent Latham, *God Is Not . . . Religious, Nice, "One of Us," An American, A Capitalist* (Grand Rapids, Mich.: Brazos Press, 2004), 129.

7. Michael Budde, cited in Brent Latham, *God Is Not . . .*, 79.

8. Tim Costello, cited in Frost and Hirsch, *Shaping of Things to Come*, 33.

9. Frost and Hirsch, *Shaping of Things to Come*, 41.

10. Ibid., 42.

11. Snyder, *The Problem of Wineskins*, 69–73.

12. Avery Dulles, *Models of the Church* (New York: Doubleday Books, 2002), 55.

13. St. Augustine, cited in James F. White, *Introduction to Christian Worship* (Nashville: Abingdon Press, 1983), 173.

14. Latham, *God Is Not . . .*, 129.

The Church Jesus Builds Is
ESCHATOLOGICAL

Joseph Coleson

Behold, I make all things new.

—Revelation 21:5 (KJV)

Nay, but there will be a greater deliverance than all this; for there will be
no more sin. And, to crown all, there will be a deep, an intimate, an unin-
terrupted union with God; a constant communion with the Father and his
Son Jesus Christ, through the Spirit; a continual enjoyment of the Three-
One God, and of all the creatures in him!

—John Wesley, Sermon LXIV, "The New Creation"

Since the slow, dusty trudge of the Eleven back to Jerusalem from the Mount of Olives where they had seen Him ascend into heaven, the Church has looked forward to Jesus' return. He promised to return, and some in every generation have thought theirs would be the one to hear the archangel's trumpet blast and see Jesus split the clouds to assume His rightful, glorious, eternal reign. The church Jesus builds is eschatological because Jesus promised to return.

What do we mean by this statement? What should we mean by this statement? Why and how is it important? In conservative Christianity, we are accustomed to thinking of the Eschaton as a sort of gateway between the times—the "end times" of our age and the beginning of the next, that is, of eternity, or perhaps of the millennium.

But we must derive the real meaning of eschatology principally from the Bible itself and from the maturing biblical understanding of the Church since the New Testament era. The Bible's own emphasis is not a focus on "the end times," but on the hope embodied in the "already and not yet" character of life with Jesus and Jesus' people. We are to express and live out this hope now, intentionally and actively, in the period before His promised return.

While the Bible's *own* emphasis is on the expression of the eschatological hope, we could go further and say that the major theme of the Bible is its eschatological promise, fulfilled in the person and redemptive work of Jesus.

This promise was prefigured in the preparation of a people to whom and through whom the Promised One would come; Jesus said as much when He told His interlocutors to search the Scriptures, for they speak of Him. The eschatological promise was fulfilled initially — and, in a very real sense, completely — in the birth, life, teaching, death, and resurrection of Jesus, who is himself the Eschaton, as revealed in His self-proclaimed title, the Alpha and Omega. Finally, the eschatological promise will be realized fully, gloriously, and eternally when Jesus fulfills His promise to return bodily to this earth and inaugurate His eternal reign of righteousness and peace.

THE OLD TESTAMENT AS ESCHATOLOGICAL PROMISE AND PREPARATION

Such a sweeping claim must be demonstrated, not merely asserted. A complete biblical hermeneutic is not satisfied with two or three proof texts, presented without regard to their immediate or larger contexts. A full treatment would require several books, not merely a single chapter, but we may consider enough here to establish that eschatology is not merely incidental in Scripture and is not concerned solely with the "time of the end." To begin this study, we will need to go back to the beginning, to a few important early episodes in salvation history (*heilsgeschichte*).

EDEN, ABRAHAM, SINAI

In Eden itself, God confronted the first couple and indicated to them some of the consequences of what they had thought was their declaration of both independence from God and equality with Him. But before speaking to them, God addressed the serpent with the curse that also contained the wondrous eschatological promise to the woman: her seed would crush the serpent's head. They could not know it at the time, of course, but that promise was the beginning of explicit biblical eschatology.

In God's initial call to Abraham, God promised him not just personal blessing and favor, but that through him all the families of the earth would be blessed and would bless themselves (Gen. 12:3). It is noteworthy that God repeated this promise to Abraham and Isaac together immediately after the near-sacrifice of Isaac (Gen. 22:18), and again to Jacob as he fled the land of promise to escape his brother Esau's lethal revenge (Gen. 28:14).

The covenant at Sinai was a further eschatological step, as God offered himself to Israel "for a God" and took Israel "for a people" (Exod. 6:7; 19:5–6; 20:2). This formula, in whole or in part, is repeated many times throughout Scripture. By the end of the New Testament, Paul, Peter, and John (at least) had applied it to those who belong to what Paul called "the Israel of God." This family of Abraham's children includes all—both Jews and Gentiles—who accept God's offer of adoption, mediated through the sacrifice of our Elder Brother, Hero, and Redeemer, Jesus the *Mashiach*, the Christ.

THE PROPHETS

As one representative of the message of all the prophets, Isaiah spoke eschatologically in many places. One of the clearest, most lyrical, and most powerful is Isaiah's heralding the coming of the Prince of the Four Names (Isa. 9:1–7). This passage begins with the promise that the people who sat in darkness would see a great light. The Israelites of the entire Galilee region were the first to lose the light of living politically as part of the people of God when, around 732 B.C., the Assyrians took all of northern Israel from Samaria's control and established provinces ruled by Assyrian governors. About a decade later, Samaria fell, the Northern Kingdom was dissolved completely, and many citizens of the remaining, truncated Israel (old Ephraim and Manasseh) were deported eastward.

But Isaiah had made a promise. North Israel's inhabitants were indeed the first to fall into darkness, but they were not deported on any great scale. Nearly eight centuries later, their descendants were the first to see the light as Jesus' earthly ministry centered in Galilee, precisely in those regions that had been first to fall under the darkness of pagan political control.

The prophecy of Jeremiah is also eschatological in much of its import, even when that prophet of Jerusalem's doom was speaking most severely to his own, mostly faithless generation. An important example is Jeremiah 29:11. Recently, many have taken this verse as a word of personal promise, with a focus on God's statement, "I know the plans I have for you." But this statement occurs in a letter Jeremiah wrote to those already exiled to Babylon, even before the fall of Jerusalem to Nebuchadnezzar's armies in 586 B.C. The last part of this verse is the important part: God's promise, "to give you a hope."

Under these circumstances, this promise was most definitely for an eschatological hope. God was not finished with the people of Judah, despite their faithlessness toward Him. God would bring a remnant home, establish them securely again in their own land, and fulfill the eternal eschatological promise through them and their descendants. As hopeful as it was to that first generation to hear Jeremiah's letter read in their assembly, it would have been no hope at all had it been a word only to them, had it contained no future hope for God's people and God's intended salvation.

This eschatological hope is seen throughout the prophets: Isaiah's call to comfort Jerusalem, his promises that the wolf and the lamb shall lie down together, that the "youngster" shall be pitied who dies at one hundred years of age, and that God will swallow up death (at the eschatological banquet, no less); Jeremiah's purchase, or redemption, of his cousin's field in Anathoth, and his promise of a fixed end to the Exile, together with God's judgment upon Babylon, who had acted too enthusiastically her part as God's instrument of judgment upon His people; Hosea's promise that God would bring Israel again into the wilderness and there "allure" her (we may as well translate this as "seduce"—a stunning thought, except that God is absolutely faithful); Joel's promise, and Peter's use of it as his text at the first Pentecost, that God would pour out His Spirit upon all humankind; Amos's vision of the plowman overtaking the reaper because of the abundant harvest; Jonah's unwilling offer of salvation both to pagan seamen and pagan empire-builders; Micah's promise to little, insignificant Bethlehem-Judah; Nahum's, Habakkuk's, and Zephaniah's promises that evil empires meet their doom; Zechariah's vision of the peaceful Ruler riding into Jerusalem on a donkey's colt; and Malachi's promise of the way-crier, figured as Elijah. I could go on for pages and only begin! The Torah, the Prophets, the Writings are all eschatological. God was preparing, has prepared, is preparing, has brought in, is bringing in, will bring in, His everlasting kingdom of righteousness and peace. All wrongs will be righted, all ills and harms healed.

CANONICAL ARRANGEMENT

Even the arrangement of the Old Testament canon has eschatological implications. The arrangement most Protestant Christians are familiar with originated with the Greek translation of the third century B.C., usually referred to as the Septuagint. This arrangement ends with Malachi, the last of the Twelve, or Minor Prophets. Malachi concludes with the promise that in that day, the Son of Righteousness would arise with healing in His wings. Most likely, it has been since Jesus' own discourse with Cleopas and his companion on the Emmaus Road that Christians have taken this promise eschatologically, as a reference to Jesus himself.

The Hebrew Bible (Jewish) arrangement of the Tanach, or Old Testament, ends with the book of Second Chronicles. Its last report is of Cyrus' edict allowing the Jewish exiles to return to their homeland if they wished, fulfilling Jeremiah's promise that Zion's judgment would have an end. The chronicler compiled his history in the post-exilic period of the beginnings of this return, and clearly intended this hopeful note to sound the eschatological theme that God will never abandon His people.

TWO COMPETING META-NARRATIVES

Before considering the New Testament's eschatological purview, I would invite you to back up with me for a few moments and consider the issue from a wider angle. (Some may say an angle wider than the scope of Hebrew/Christian eschatology is impossible; I may be inclined to agree, but that is another matter for another time.) This "wider angle" is the (relatively) recently popularized concept of meta-narrative. Meta-narrative is "the big story" of a people, of a nation, or of a civilization. The stories told as history, or in explanation of a people's character or "personality," are a part of their meta-narrative.

The national meta-narrative of the United States includes the stories of John Smith and Pocahontas; the Pilgrims, Squanto, and the first Thanksgiving; Valley Forge and Yorktown; Lincoln, Grant, and Lee; Pearl Harbor, Normandy, and Iwo Jima; Armstrong on the moon; cowboys and baseball; and of our universal immigrant status, from the first who crossed the Bering Strait ice bridge, to those who've arrived today. Canada's meta-narrative includes French and British exploration, rivalry, settlement, and several wars; First Nations; Dominion and British Commonwealth status; cold, snow, and ice hockey; and the RCMP (Royal Canadian Mounted Police). Every people, nation, and civilization has its own meta-narrative, its stories connected as "the big story" that explains where they came from and why, and where they hope the future will take them.

For the world as a whole today, there are only two competing meta-narratives. Most simply stated, one meta-narrative declares the existence of a transcendent God, and the other denies the existence of a transcendent God. That is the only real, significant choice among the myriad of belief systems present in the world today.

THE TWO META-NARRATIVES DEFINED

Christianity and Judaism start from the belief that a single, personal, transcendent God created all else that exists. This and all it entails is one meta-narrative. All other belief systems of our world, whether presented as theologies, or as religious or secular philosophical systems, ultimately deny the existence of a transcendent personal deity, making the universe itself, or some aspects of it, the measure of all. That is, they are ultimately naturalistic. This and all it entails is the other meta-narrative. Because "all it entails" is quite a lot in both meta-narratives, we often don't recognize that these are the only two.

THE "HAS GOD REALLY SAID?" META-NARRATIVE

The second, naturalistic meta-narrative has several dominant forms in today's world. Some forms of the second meta-narrative posit personalistic deities, either one or more, but the deities posited are not the God revealed in the Judeo-Christian Scriptures. Other forms of the second meta-narrative teach that the ultimate destiny of all life is to merge back into the spiritual, non-personal essence from which it emerged. Essentially, this is a Gnostic, non-personal dualism; some of its strains have seemingly Christian colorations. Still other forms of the second meta-narrative dispense with any deity at all, and teach an entirely naturalistic understanding of the universe. With all that accompanies each, these systems seem to be different, even competing and conflicting, ideologies, but at their foundation—the denial of a single, personal, transcendent God—they all are but variations on a single theme, one meta-narrative in several recensions.

GOD'S META-NARRATIVE

The first meta-narrative is God's, primarily. It is ours, secondarily, not because we invented it, but because we have been invited into it and have accepted God's gracious invitation. It relates the story of the one God who existed and exists before all, in the fellowship of perfect community within the triune Godhead of Father, Son, and Holy Spirit. Not needing, but desiring, further relationships within which to express the love that characterizes the Godhead, God created all else that is. On this earth, the culmination of God's loving creation is the being whom God named 'adam, or human.

The first two of 'adam rejected God's fellowship and community, thinking they could get along on their own—in fact, could be gods themselves. God did not reject them, however, but put into motion a plan to redeem 'adam and restore the relationship that both God and 'adam enjoyed before the break theologians often call "the Fall" (Gen. 5:2).

The narrative thread of what Christians call the Old Testament concerns the outworking of God's plan to prepare a people through whom this redemption and restoration could be realized. Though this point often is forgotten or ignored, the promised restoration of God's created order was never intended to be limited to this one people, but was to be for all peoples *through* them.

The heart of this meta-narrative is the Incarnation: the birth, life, teaching, death, and resurrection of Jesus, the Christ, the Son of God, the second person of the triune Godhead. His redeeming death was a catastrophe, a shattering event of not merely terrestrial, but cosmic, import. But it was a *good* catastrophe, what Tolkien called a "eucatastrophe." In fact, it is the most important eucatastrophe beside which all others, from any and all stories whatsoever, pale in significance. Read in Tolkien's own words:

> [The Gospels] contain many marvels . . . and among the marvels is the greatest and most complete conceivable eucatastrophe. But this story has entered History and the primary world; . . . The Resurrection is the eucatastrophe of the story of the Incarnation. This story begins and ends in joy. It has pre-eminently the "inner consistency of reality." There is no tale ever told that men would rather find was true, and none which so many skeptical men have accepted as true on its own merits. For the Art of it has the supremely convincing tone of Primary Art, that is, of Creation. To reject it leads either to sadness or to wrath. . . .
>
> . . . The Christian joy, the Gloria, is . . . pre-eminently (infinitely, if our capacity were not finite) high and joyous. But this story is supreme; and it is true.[1]

Tolkien here identifies the Hebrew/Christian meta-narrative as the great, the only, eucatastrophe — of all stories, the one most important to be "real," the one we hope most fervently is "real," the one which must be "real" if life is to have ultimate meaning. At its center, this is the eucatastrophe Tolkien's friend C. S. Lewis described in *The Lion, the Witch, and the Wardrobe* as the willing death of an innocent victim in a traitor's stead, the death that began death itself working backward to resurrection for all who will accept the offer of divine friendship—indeed, of divine sonship/daughterhood.[2]

The rest of the New Testament documents the beginning of the Fellowship of the Redeemed, which we call (because the New Testament calls it) the Church of Jesus Christ. It is this Church that continues today, and will continue forever, so that all the history of the Church from then on is a part of the great meta-narrative.

It is important to note that the concept of meta-narrative is itself eschatological, especially when applied to God's plan of redemption and the resulting family of faith called "the Church." In the Gospels of the New Testament, Jesus repeatedly told those He spoke with that the kingdom of heaven was "at hand." That is the language of immediacy; Jesus was telling His hearers that the Eschaton had (at least, nearly) arrived. Its arrival is seen in Jesus' death and resurrection, and in the establishment of the Church on the day of Pentecost. The Eschaton is already here, though we do not yet see all it will be and all it will bring. This way of understanding the Eschaton, centered in Jesus Christ, as the point and purpose of God's meta-narrative, merits further consideration.

AN ESCHATOLOGICAL FAMILY

Jesus said more than once in His earthly ministry that the kingdom of heaven was (and is) "at hand," "at the door," and other similar phrasings. But then He also said that only God the Father knows the time of His return, the *parousia*, as it is called in the disciplines of New Testament and systematic theology.

So what can we know, and how can we know it, especially in light of the many times various individuals or groups within the Church have figured out that Jesus' coming must occur on such-and-such a day, only to have the anticipated day come and go, and all things continue as they always have?

As it often occurs, in trying to figure out what Jesus meant, or what some other portion of Scripture meant and means, we have understood both too much and too little of His, and their, teaching. We have understood too much in hearing Jesus' words that state that considerable upheavals of various kinds will precede and accompany His return (as befit the coming of great royalty), which results in our reading into every set of unusual phenomena in the heavens, the earth, the seas, and the politics of the world, foreshadowings of His immediate descent. We have understood too little in not perceiving that by "at the door" and "at hand" Jesus meant that the Kingdom is already among us or, rather, that we are already in the Kingdom, that the Eschaton is here.

TOO MUCH OF "THE DAY"

If all we think we need to do is tally up the signs—and too often that has been our only hermeneutical strategy—then we can already find most of the "signs of the times" that are often cited as proof that the "end times" are near or here, documented in world history since Jesus' ascension. Jesus' teaching in Matthew 24, Mark 13, and Luke 21 was largely fulfilled in the siege and destruction of Jerusalem by the Roman legions under Titus from A.D. 67–70. The oft-referenced chapters of Daniel were fulfilled even earlier, beginning in the time of the Maccabees, then in and through Jesus' own sacrificial death. By the checklist method of interpreting prophecy, not much is left for the end, yet this method demands many phenomena as the signs of the "end times."

THE ONE IMPORTANT "SIGN"

Yet there is one supremely important "sign." Presently, it rests only and completely in God's own mind and will. In Jesus' teaching known as the Olivet Discourse, he said the angels of heaven do not know, *not even He himself knows*, the day of His return; only the Father knows (Mark 13:32). Why does Jesus not know? How could Jesus not know? The reason is both astounding and heartwarming.

The answer lies in a set of marriage customs observed in first-century Judaism, at least in its homeland. Most marriages were arranged, with the fathers of the bride and groom taking the principal parts in the negotiations. Once the fathers, the bride, and the groom all agreed to the wedding and its terms, the bride and groom were espoused. Breaking the agreement required a divorce, though the groom continued to live in his father's house or on his estate, and the bride continued to live with her parents.

The bride's responsibility was to collect and organize her trousseau, then to be ready at a few moments' notice for whenever her groom would arrive to take her to their new home, where the wedding would be celebrated. Meanwhile, the groom was back home with his father. He was charged with building a new home, either an apartment within or added onto his father's home, or a new house on his father's estate. It is not uncommon to see a variant of this practice in the modern Middle East. Often, a newly married couple will occupy a floor above the groom's parents in a multi-story home. Several sons may live with their families on several floors, above their parents, who reside on the ground floor.

But if the groom's task was to prepare a home for himself and his bride, who decided when that new home was ready? It should come as no surprise to learn that the groom was not allowed to make that decision. Grooms have a tendency to want to bring their brides home; grooms could be tempted to take shortcuts to speed the building along. The decision that the new home was ready, that it was suitable for the newlywed couple, belonged to the father of the groom. When he pronounced it finished, the groom could go for his bride at her home, and the wedding celebration could begin.

Jesus told the Eleven in the Upper Room that on His Father's estate are many dwelling places. He said that He was going to prepare a place for them and for all who would be wooed to Him in the future and become a part of His Bride, the Church (John 14:2–3). But even the Heavenly Groom does not get to decide when that place is ready. That decision is the Father's. This is why Jesus said only the Father knows the day and hour of His return, because only the Father knows when the palace and estate will be ready to receive the Heavenly Bride.

Jesus rescued and ransomed us, redeemed and delivered us, at the price of His own blood. He makes us pure and spotless, clothed in garments of pure white. He labors now to prepare our heavenly home. When the Father says to Him, "Now, Son, it's ready; you may go and bring your Bride," Jesus' friend and attendant, the archangel, will blow the trumpet, and our Groom will ride to receive us on His white horse. We will go with Him to the home He personally has prepared, and so shall we ever be with the Lord, our Elder Brother, our Hero, our Beloved Bridegroom.

It will happen in the moment the Father says, "Son, it's ready; Son, it's time." It will not happen because someone here on earth has figured out the signs. Our assignment is to be ready. We can be ready by being faithful to the King and serious about the business of the Kingdom to which we have been appointed.

NOT ENOUGH OF "THE KINGDOM IS HERE ALREADY"

I am writing the bulk of this chapter at Christmastide. Let me ask you to picture yourself as a child approaching the Christmas tree as the family gathers to unwrap the gifts. You take your turns opening yours, along with everyone else. Each gift is *better* than the last, and *exactly* what you wanted, and *more* than you ever dreamed, all at the same time. Finally, you come to the last gift; it's bigger than any of the others, wrapped more beautifully than any gift you have ever seen, and when you open it, for a moment you truly cannot believe your parents have given it to you.

What is this gift? I don't know what yours would be; I can only guess at my own. My point is that when the Eschaton is fully unwrapped, when we realize that our invitation to be an eternal part of it is real—that it can never be rescinded or jeopardized, that we never have to be out of God's glorious, holy presence again—our joy will be like the young lad or lass who has just opened the best Christmas present ever, because, in a very real sense, that is exactly what we just will have done.

But we're not finished. Picture yourself as the father or mother of that child who has just experienced the best Christmas ever. If you've been there, you know that the joy of securing, wrapping, and placing that gift under the Christmas tree is as beyond the receiving of gifts as the full, unclouded moon is beyond a single candle.

Jesus said in Luke 11 (and I'm paraphrasing a bit, as you will recognize) that if we, being fallen creatures with hardly ever an entirely pure motive to even our smallest acts of kindness, can give good gifts to our children, how much more will our Father lavish upon us heavenly, eternal gifts that we cannot begin to imagine here below? And if we rejoice in our children's joy as they receive our gifts, how much greater is God's delight and joy at the unending rapture of His children as we open His gifts throughout eternity, as children welcomed into the very family of God?

This is what eschatology is. *This* is what the Church is to be about, because the Eschaton has already begun. It began no later than the moment Peter stepped out upon the balcony of that Upper Room in Jerusalem on the Day of Pentecost and proclaimed to the wondering crowd below, "This is that which was spoken by the prophet Joel" (Acts 2:16, KJV). The kingdom of God is among us. The Church is not the entirety of the Kingdom, but it is a central part of the Kingdom. As many have said, the Kingdom is already, as well as not yet. It is time the Church began to live in the "already" at least as much as we live in the "not yet." As it is the loving parent's good pleasure to give the child good gifts so, Jesus said, it is the Father's good pleasure to give us the Kingdom. Let us begin to live in the reality of what we have already received.

The greatest gift we can receive beyond the Kingdom, though, is God's own self. Truly we shall, in the end, cast before God our crowns and all our other gifts, great and small, and in the splendor, comfort, and inexpressible joy of God's own presence, forevermore be lost in wonder, love, and grace—not as remote citizens of the Kingdom, but as intimate members of the Heavenly Royal Family. Why shouldn't we begin to live it in the here and now?

SO WHAT DOES THIS LOOK LIKE IN MY CHURCH?

What was Jesus' own instruction to His people awaiting the day of His return? For He did tell us to expect His return. He advised us to watch, but not as those who spend their days idly looking eastward to see some change in the sky.

FAITHFULNESS

Our watching is to be the watching of the faithful servant engaged in his or her appointed tasks upon the Master's estate. If we are stable hands, we are to put down straw and feed, exercise and groom the stock, muck out the stalls and the gutters.

If we are scullery maids, we are to be peeling the potatoes, scrubbing the pots and pans, and mopping the floors. If our task is to keep the books, we ought not to pretend to be the steward who gives out the daily assignments to the laborers. If we are the tutor to the Master's underage children, we need to be content to wait for the Master to return and release us from our familiar schoolroom with its dusty chalkboard.

We are to be faithful to our appointed tasks, whatever they may be, however onerous or honorable. We are not to be lounging out by the road at the end of the lane, endlessly speculating whether today, tomorrow, or next week, will be the day of the Master's return. Those whom the Master will praise as faithful will be those who actually are in the stable, the field, the scullery, the classroom, or the bookkeeping office, doing what He has equipped and appointed them to do.

Yet, as paradoxical as it may seem, we are to do all this with at least the occasional eye to the eastern sky, at least the occasional whispered longing, "Oh, Lord, let it be today!" It is right that the Church and all its members individually should love His appearing — that is, long for His return. We long for mortal loved ones when they are absent from us for an extended time. It is not wrong, but decidedly right, to long for the return of the One whom we have never yet seen, but whom upon seeing, we shall know instantly.

Faithfulness is *not* an abstraction. Faithfulness is the *sine qua non* of every relationship, required of all parties in the relationship. God's faithful love calls us to faithfulness to himself and to His people; God's grace makes our faithfulness possible. As ministers and leaders in the church, we are to model and encourage faithfulness constantly (a synonym of *faithfulness* is *constancy*). Your individual act and attitude of faithfulness will not always duplicate mine, but let me suggest three areas in which, I believe, the kind of eschatologically informed faithfulness we have been discussing will bear much fruit in the local church—the Church Jesus is building of which we both are a part.

SACRAMENTAL CELEBRATION

Families with warm, loving histories together have rituals that gain in meaning and importance over the years. The Church is a family, too, and our rituals include the sacraments. Various branches of the family count their number differently, administer them differently (a few, not at all), and assess their efficacy in different ways. But even those who do not administer the sacraments at all acknowledge the importance of the concepts they are intended to teach and the family life they celebrate.

As leaders in a sacramental church, we have the responsibility and privilege of teaching and celebrating the sacraments as initiation, as marks of initiation, and as remembrance of our initiation into the kingdom and family of God. In our Catholic/Anglican/Methodist tradition, baptism is the initiation into the family. Every baptism should be a joyous celebration of that for the one baptized, and a "birthday" celebration for those in attendance. That is why the more traditional baptismal liturgies include the admonition, "Remember your [own] baptism."

The term *Eucharist* is from the Greek root that expresses thanksgiving, or thankfulness. In Greece today, when one receives a service, a gift, or a favor, the proper response is *efcharisto*, another form from this root. The Eucharist, or Lord's Supper, is a thanksgiving meal instituted by Jesus himself, with the invitation to celebrate it often: "Do this, *whenever* you drink it, in remembrance of me" (1 Cor. 11:25, emphasis added). The bread and the blood of the grape are immediate and vivid reminders of what it cost Jesus to secure our membership in His family, as His younger brothers and sisters.

We have the privilege of serving this sober, joyous meal to our brothers and sisters. For many of us so privileged, over the years, it has become (as it was for Wesley) a precious occasion, its meaning growing deeper over time, its lack sorely felt when we are too long absent from the Table. Let us be diligent to help others experience often, and grow to value, this family ritual instituted by our Elder Brother himself. It is both a sign of, and an active participation in, our status as loved and valued members of the family.

PREACHING

In our preaching and teaching ministries, it is vitally important that we keep this eschatological frame of reference, mindset, and atmosphere always before our people. It is not that we have to use the word *eschatological* in every utterance, but even without using the word or preaching always from overtly eschatological texts, we need to cultivate, model, and encourage ourselves and God's people to think, live, act, and speak eschatologically.

Too much preaching today focuses on "Five Steps to Pain-free Living in *This* World." But we are on an eschatological journey *through,* and ultimately *from,* the brokenness of this present world. True, the Eschaton has arrived, but it also is not yet. We are citizens of the heavenly kingdom, but we also are sojourners in this world, which has not yet experienced its full redemption. Until then, the paradigms of this world are not the paradigms of the Kingdom. Only by living as God's Royal Family, in this world but not of it, will we live consistently the full, joyous, open, generous, and faithful lives that reflect the character of God.

EVANGELIZATION

Such lives also will tend to draw others from the darkness of this fallen world into the glorious light of God's presence. The work of evangelism is, at its best and deepest, the introduction to, invitation to, and initiation of others into the kingdom and family of God.

Mere "morality models" will not suffice, neither for ourselves nor for those who are observing, whom we are hoping to help enter the family. Morality cannot be the engine of our evangelism, but only a freight car pulled by the engine of love. God's love for us, demonstrated before a shocked universe in the bleeding sacrifice that ghastly, beautiful day at Calvary, is the only adequate motivator of right living for a race created with the capacity for, and granted the privilege of, making our own decisions.

Once captivated by that glorious passion of God, we will make the moral decisions and be eager all our lives to learn how to do it better. It is the difference between living in the exuberance of love and fulfilling the drudgery of hated obligation—and, all too often, the world knows it better than we do. In the end, the faithful, hope-filled, loving life of a liberated daughter or son of the Most High is not only the most fulfilling life there can be, but it will also prove irresistible to many who are disillusioned by this world's shallow cuteness.

Pastor, preacher, teacher, church leader, new member of the family: Live! Rejoice! Live in the joy of the already and the anticipation of the not yet. Live for our Bridegroom, for He is coming! On that glorious day, God will wipe away every tear from every face, and so shall we ever be with the Lord. Even so, come, Lord Jesus.

ACTION SUGGESTIONS

1. Find and read Tolkien's essay, "On Fairy Stories." Study especially the last six pages or so. It will stimulate your thinking on God's gifts of joy, as few other readings, thoughts, or events will.

2. Read, re-read, ponder, and preach Isaiah 25:6–9 together with Revelation 21:1–7. Your people need this hopeful preaching. (If you preach through to the end of both these pericopes, notice that those who are left out of the banquet are out due to their own choice, not God's choice.)

3. Scan this chapter again. What grabs your attention? Ponder, appropriate, and preach that!

FOR FURTHER READING

Lewis, C. S. *The Last Battle: The Chronicles of Narnia*. New York: HarperCollins Publishers, 2001.

Lewis's imaginative fiction remains a rich source of catalytic situations, events, and imagery for the Christian communicator. We would do well to emulate Lewis in our passion to portray the depth and breadth of the joy we (should) have in the hope of Christ's return. Yes, Jesus is more than Lewis's Aslan, but He surely is not less.

Moltmann, Jürgen. *Theology of Hope*. Minneapolis: Fortress Press, 1993.

Moltmann, in this work particularly, is credited with making the subject of eschatology "respectable" in current systematic theology. Moltmann can be "heavy going" in places, but a few pages, now and then, of "heavy going" should be a welcome exercise for the pastor and proclaimer of the Word, should it not?

Tolkien, J. R. R. "On Fairy Stories," *The Tolkien Reader*. New York: Del Rey, 2002.

"On Fairy Stories" is the full essay from which the Tolkien quotation found in this chapter is drawn. Every Christian can profit from reading and pondering this extraordinary essay. For the pastor or for any Christian communicator, I would rate it as well-nigh indispensable for Tolkien's treatment of the great work of "sub-creation" to which we are called.

Wesley, John. Sermon LX: "The General Deliverance" and Sermon LXIV: "The New Creation." These sermons are available in a number of places, but most conveniently at http://gbgm-umc.org/UMHISTORY/Wesley/sermons/.

Wesley's texts for these two sermons are Romans 8:19–22 and Revelation 21:5, respectively. If you have thought of the principal founder of Methodism as dour and joyless, think again. In these two sermons, Wesley revels in God's grand design for the restoration of all creation, already accomplished in Jesus' death and resurrection, but to be experienced fully only at the end of time as we now live it.

Wesley, John. Several others of Wesley's sermons are useful, in whole or in part, on the subject of biblical eschatology, rightly understood as the entirety of God's plan to rescue and restore the whole of creation in and through the redemptive work of Christ. Among these are Sermon LIV: "On Eternity"; Sermon XCIX: "The Reward of the Righteous"; Sermon CIII: "What Is Man?"; Sermon CIX: "What Is Man?" (a different sermon of the same title); Sermon CXXIX: "The Cause and Cure of Earthquakes"; Sermon CXXXVII: "On the Resurrection of the Dead" (a sermon abridged and revised by Wesley from a sermon by Benjamin Calamy). These also are available at the web site noted above. You may not (I don't) agree with every point Mr. Wesley makes, but these sermons will greatly stimulate your thinking.

NOTES

1. J. R. R. Tolkien, "On Fairy-Stories" in *Tree and Leaf*, repr. in *The Tolkien Reader* (New York: Ballantine Books, 1966), 71–72.

2. C. S. Lewis, *The Lion, the Witch, and the Wardrobe*: *The Chronicles of Narnia* (New York: HarperCollins Publishers, 2001), 185.

3

The Church Jesus Builds Is

HOLY

Keith Drury

But you are a chosen people, a royal priesthood, a holy nation, a people belonging to God, that you may declare the praises of him who called you out of darkness into his wonderful light. Once you were not a people, but now you are the people of God.

—1 Peter 2:9–10

The Bible knows nothing of solitary religion. . . . There is no holiness but social holiness.

—John Wesley

W hen those of us in holiness churches hear the word *holiness*, we usually think of personal holiness more than corporate holiness. When we do this, we make a big mistake. Of all people, those of us in holiness churches should grasp and treasure the idea of a holy *people*, not just holy persons. Holiness churches should be just that— holiness *churches*, not merely a collection of individual holy people.

IF EVERY INDIVIDUAL IS HOLY, WON'T THAT MAKE A HOLY CHURCH?

It seems reasonable to think that if every individual in a church were a holy person, then we would have a holy church, but it doesn't work that way. The whole is greater than the sum of the parts. One good man and one good woman and two good children do not automatically make a good *family*. They might be wonderful individuals, yet a family is much more than a collection of wonderful persons. Indeed, it is possible to be four wonderful persons, yet not even have a real family.

To use another example, it takes more than two individuals who have experienced a civil or religious ceremony to make a marriage. A genuine marriage—as God instituted it and the Bible and Christian tradition both envision it—also requires love and commitment, and can be entered into by only one man with one woman, one woman with one man. All who experience it know that in a genuine marriage, the whole is greater than the sum of the parts.

As with the family and with marriage, so a holy church is more than a collection of individuals who are holy persons. In fact, it even is possible for holy *individuals* to come together as a church body, and *as a group*, and act far less than holy.

GROUPS CAN SIN

We need only to turn to the Bible to understand this idea: a group can sin as a group, and a group can be righteous as a group. The nation of Israel was at times pronounced righteous by God, and at other times they were collectively condemned. While some of this condemnation for sin was a result of God adding up all the personal sins, in other cases it seems to have been because God rejected the people as a whole, due to their collective national attitudes. A person can be arrogant and self-reliant, and so can a nation. While an individual holds some personal responsibility for corporate sin, it is possible for the individual to be relatively innocent (personally), yet still the collective people are judged and the innocent suffer too. Not every member of Achan's family was guilty of avarice and disobedience, yet they all suffered for his sin. Certainly, at least a few good

Judeans lived in or around Jerusalem when God punished them all and allowed the Babylonians to take them away into exile. God relates to individuals, but God also relates to *groups* of people—as groups—including families, tribes, and nations. God relates to you and me personally, but He also relates to us as a group—and today the primary group God works with is the Church.

A church can sin as a group even when many (perhaps all) in the church do not personally and willfully participate. Such corporate sins often are attitudes and sins of omission, but these also can be detrimental to God's will for His church. When everybody is responsible, nobody is responsible. So sometimes we stand back and allow the church to sin as a group while we personally do nothing. But we are responsible as a group—for God not only punishes sinning individuals, but He also punishes sinning groups. And when the church, *as a group*, sins, it is a serious matter.

GROUPS CAN BE HOLY

A group also can be holy, as a group. The Church is supposed to be a holy people. A church can act Christlike—*as a group*—in ways an individual cannot. What individual among us would claim to be a perfect example of all the characteristics of Christlikeness? Who would say, "Here, look at me, and you will find a perfect example of Christ's mercy, grace, compassion, tenderness, justice, wisdom, and suffering"? Would *you*? Well, *would* you?

See? Not one of us in our right minds would claim to be an example of all these qualities of Christ. Yet we can find each of them in the church collectively. There may be only two or three people in any congregation who model Christlike compassion for the poor and disenfranchised, but you can find them in the church. There may be only a single person in a congregation who exhibits a Christlike passion for the lost, but you can find her in the church.

It is in the church that we find Christlikeness in its fullest sense. This is why we never consider ourselves individually to be the "body of Christ." Would you? Never! I am not the body of Christ. Neither are you. *We* are the body of Christ. All of us Christians in the Church collectively are Christ's body. Together we can find among us all the character qualities of Jesus Christ. While no one of us perfectly exhibits all these qualities, together in the power of the Spirit, we show the world what Jesus Christ is like, for we are His body.

OUR INDIVIDUALISTIC MIND-SET

Every cell in our individualistic minds rebels at this idea. From childhood, our culture trains us to refuse to melt, to be a stand-alone individual. Television shows and movies lionize individuals who claim, "I did it my way." The theater constantly throws forth heroes who buck the system, ignore the group, and live by their own standards. We are discipled by our culture to demand our own rights, to get what we want, and to make our desires known as angry customers who will threaten to take our business elsewhere if our demands are not met. This is how we are raised in the Western world—especially in North America. It leaks into our religion as well, for it is hard to have a religion that departs too far from the culture's values. This is why we come to worship like customers insisting on having the meal served exactly to our liking.

So we have *personal* devotions, *personal* mentoring, and *personal* time alone with God as we elevate the privatization of religion and marginalize the Church. One popular student Facebook® group on a Christian college campus is named "We Love Jesus but Hate the Church." What kind of Christians are these? However, these students merely went to the logical end of the privatized personalized religion of their parents. When personal devotions become more important than corporate worship, when personal deeds become more important than the church's group service, when private time alone with

70

God is elevated while the Christ-established corporate sacraments are lightly dismissed, this is what we get a generation later: people who claim to love Jesus and hate His body.

But it can't be done. We can't behead Jesus and reject the rest of his body. There are no real Christians who hate the Church, for how can someone love Christ, whom they have not seen, if they do not love His body, which they can see?

ONE HOLY CHURCH

So, the Church is a group, a community. We have noted above that just as a group can sin *as a group*, so a group also can be holy *as a group*. Some individual churches are holy and others aren't. Is your local church *one holy church*? If not, it can be. Indeed, the New Testament continually urges the Church to become a holy Church. It calls us collectively to be sanctified and purified.

In our individualized culture we have a hard time reading the Bible for what it says. We read our own assumptions *into* the Bible. For instance, when the Bible says, "You be holy," we immediately take the *you* to mean *me*. In English, *you* can be taken as a singular or a plural, but our culture trains us to read *you* in the Bible as singular—me personally. Yet in the Bible, most of the commands to be holy are plural—plural instructions to the Church as a group to be holy. How holiness churches have missed this emphasis for so long escapes us all, but it is clearly the teaching of Scripture. God wants a holy people, and He won't get this just by making individuals holy; He wants to sanctify the Church collectively too.

HOW CAN A CHURCH BECOME HOLY?

Most of us can understand the idea of corporate sin more easily than we can comprehend corporate holiness, but *groups* can be holy, just as they can be sinful. What is holiness? It is Christlikeness—living in word, thought, and deed as Jesus would live, relying on the power of the Holy Spirit. Holiness is loving and serving others, worshipping God, being easily entreated, hungering for more of God, avoiding disobedience to God, reaching out to the lost and hurting. An individual can experience all of these things—but so can a group. The church can be *one holy church*.

But how? Obviously just gathering as a congregation does not make the group holy any more than attending church will make an individual holy. So how does God sanctify the church—the group? He does it through various means of grace. These are the channels of changing grace God prefers to use to make us become what we aren't yet. God uses the means of grace to mold His church, to correct her, to eliminate sin and foot-dragging, to grant us a collective passion for the lost, and to enable us to love Him, each other, and the world.

There are two categories of the means of grace: personal and corporate. Some means of grace are personal, like solitude and silence; other means of grace can only be received corporately, like the Lord's Supper. Still other means, such as prayer, fall into both the personal and the corporate categories. Just as God uses personal devotions to change us individually, He uses the corporate means of grace to change the church corporately into His Son's image.

But it is not by the means of grace alone that God changes His church, for corporate experiences also can alter the corporate soul of a church. For instance, a church can be filled with the Holy Spirit, just as an individual can be filled. We are speaking here of more than simultaneous individual fillings; God sometimes will indwell the collective body of Christ in a way He does not indwell individuals. So both the corporate means of grace and corporate experiences can sanctify a church, making it one holy church. Consider some of the following means God uses to make a holy church.

FILLING WITH THE HOLY SPIRIT

We are familiar with being personally filled with the Spirit, but few of us ever expect (or even believe) that the whole church could be filled with the Spirit. But what if we could experience this today? What if God came upon His gathered people and filled them with His Spirit? What would that be like? Well, it would be like the church in the book of Acts. When God fills His church with the Holy Spirit, that body of believers will never be the same again.

Why does this not happen today? Why is such an experience never sought or expected? We give altar calls for *individuals* to be Spirit-filled, but what if an entire congregation, all at once, sought this experience—as a church? What if we all went to the altar? Did God quit filling the church with the Spirit after the book of Acts was closed? Some of us don't think so. But most of our churches will never be Spirit-filled. Why? We only imagine that if each individual were filled with the Spirit, then when we all gather, the church itself would automatically be Spirit-filled. Thus, we do not even believe there is such a thing as the Spirit filling a *church*, so in our unbelief we get exactly what we expect. We expect nothing; we get nothing.

If we want our church to be a sanctified church, we first need to help it believe there is such a thing as a corporate filling from God, then we need to become a seeking church—seeking to be filled with God's Spirit, as a church. It's hard even to imagine, isn't it? We have so individualized and personalized the work of God that we can barely even conceive of a corporate sanctification experience. But if God would be pleased to respond to such seeking faith by instantly filling our church with the Holy Spirit in a powerful experience of grace, what would that produce? It would begin to produce *one holy church.*

MOVING OF GOD

It is easier for us to imagine a "moving of God" than a corporate filling of the Spirit. Have you ever been in a service in which God moved? Such a thing happened when they dedicated the Tabernacle. It happened again at the Temple dedication. Has it ever happened at *your* church? Have you ever seen the Spirit of God descend upon His church in a way that was undeniable and indelible? Maybe it happened during the music or maybe during the preaching or altar call, but have you ever witnessed a moving of God that could not be attributed to human manipulation or talent?

Such an experience can alter a congregation for years. When God moves among His people, they change. Collectively, not just as individuals (though that is also true), the church becomes closer to God. Some churches have to go back a long way in their history to cite a memory of God's moving. How far back does your church have to go?

THE LORD'S SUPPER

While many revivalist holiness people at least can recall things like God's "moving" among us, we often have a poorer record concerning the actual sacraments, the means of grace established by Christ himself. The service of Holy Communion is more than a remembrance for a dead man—it is a means of grace designed by God to change His Church and make her holy. John Wesley fought the lackadaisical attitude toward the Lord's Supper in his day, and we must fight it today. This attitude is expressed in statements like, "Communion takes too long," or "It isn't relevant to daily life," or "It's a downer, and we want to be brighter in our services." So we assign it to some sideshow service, which most of the people skip. Shame on us. No wonder the Church lacks holiness; it lacks one of the chief means of grace, Holy Communion.

When John Wesley was asked, "How often should I take communion?" he responded simply and directly, "As often as you can." We argue that it loses meaning if we "have it too often," yet who among us would say we should pray less in worship so prayer will not lose its meaning? Would we be willing to read Scripture only once a quarter to make sure it "doesn't lose its meaning"?

The Lord's Supper is a mystical gift from God to His Church. It cannot be practiced by an individual alone, any more than marriage can be experienced by only one person. It is a group experience, and it is a group sanctifying experience, *if* we'll let it become that. However, if to us it is nothing more than a troublesome, dead ritual, we will get nothing from it. God intends to sanctify His Church through His blood and body. If we will take it often and take it by faith, He will change us as a corporate body to become a church more like Christ. In taking the body and blood of our Lord, we increasingly become the flesh and blood representation of the body of Christ on earth. Can we take it more frequently? Can we take it believing in God's changing power through this sacrament? If we will, He will.

CONVERSION AND BAPTISM

Seeing new converts come to Christ and receiving them into the family through the sacrament of baptism is a transforming experience for any church. Too many local churches have seen too many months go by without seeing even one person converted and changed, let alone experiencing someone's baptism as an induction into the family of God. When a church sees a life changed, that church is altered. We are reminded again, "This is what it's all about." We are changed to become a more godly church—a church that values the things God values.

TESTIMONY

Hearing about God's mighty works in the lives of His people is a means of grace that God uses to sanctify the Church. Whether it is the old-fashioned personal testimony or the more modern edition of it projected on a video screen, God uses such testimonies to make His people, collectively, more like His Son. When we hear of God working in the lives of others, our own faith grows and we begin to become a believing church, expecting God to change and transform people. Without such witnesses, a church gradually forgets God's power not only to forgive but also to deliver His people from their personal flaws and sinful habits. A miraculous deliverance is wonderful to experience, but if nobody hears about it when the church is gathered together as the body of Christ, it is as useful to the body as a tree falling in the woods with nobody around to hear it.

CORPORATE PRAYER

Just as prayer is a significant personal means of grace, it also is a means through which God sanctifies the church collectively. In prayer we are melted together as one church and we learn to wait on the Lord, listening for His direction and commands. A church that uses prayer as a segue to provide cover for those on the "stage" to move to a new location will not become a holy people through prayer. Prayer is more than an oil to make the minute-by-minute worship schedule run more smoothly. It is a face-to-face encounter with God. Prayer is the church's means of approaching God's throne as a group, to lay before Him our requests, and to receive, from God, His promptings. The church that prays together stays together. And the church that prays together becomes more like Christ every time it does so. It is a means of grace through which God sanctifies the church.

SCRIPTURE

It takes very little effort to convince Protestants of the importance of the sacred Scriptures. In some ways we consider Scripture to be a greater sacrament than the actual sacraments. We treat it as the *chief* means of grace, no matter what we say in our doctrine. We may be right or wrong in this revisionist approach to the sacraments, but we certainly will agree that when God's people are gathered, the public reading of Scripture and preaching that is solidly scriptural is a means of grace for God to form His church into a holy people. Reading the Bible on our own at home is important, but even more important is listening at church to the Scripture and to the "preaching of the pure word of God." Scripture has a cleansing effect on us as we gather together that it does not have when we read it alone. While Protestants may do better at understanding the importance of Scripture as a personal means of grace, we still fall short in understanding how it is a corporate means—how God uses the Scriptures to sanctify the church, *as a church*—as we hear it read and preached.

KOINONIA

Potluck suppers and traveling together in a van to shop on a Saturday may seem mostly like fun, but activities like these are an essential corporate means of grace through which God binds His church in unity. How can we love one another if we are seldom together? "Doing life together" is an increasing theme in the emerging church, and it is sound doctrine. God sanctifies His church as we mix together. In his preaching, Steve DeNeff (pastor of College Wesleyan Church, Marion, Indiana) sometimes reminds us that the church is like God's washing machine. We all come together, and as we tumble in the washing of the Word, we experience a group cleansing. *Koinonia* denotes even more than fellowship, but just getting together is at least a start. As we gather and do life together, God uses us to encourage, correct, urge, guide and inspire one other. And from our interaction, we come away encouraged, corrected, urged, and inspired ourselves. As we fellowship together, God is in the midst of us, using each of us to help the rest of us to become more like Christ, collectively. As we do this, we gradually become in actuality what we are in name: the community of Christ.

These are just a few of the corporate means of grace by which God sanctifies His people as a group. There are others, but these are enough to awaken us to the idea of a holiness church being a *holy* church as a group. God wants to turn the gathered assembly of His people into the image of His own Son, Jesus.

TOGETHER, THE CHURCH BECOMES HOLY

All this talk about corporate sanctification may seem strange to us—even to us holiness people. But it is true. And it is biblical. While personal holiness is very important, it is not enough; God wants a holy *people*, not just holy persons. Once we see that our stubborn individuality can be a barrier to letting go and letting God work to make His gathered Church a Holy people, we can start this collective journey together. Maybe we can start to see our church as God sees it—as His chosen Bride who is being made perfect by her Heavenly Groom. None of us can personally be His Bride nor should we even want to be. But all of us *together* are the Bride of Christ. Together He wants to cleanse us, to make us spotless, to enable us to become His radiant Bride. And He does this as we are together, not as individual body parts. God will make us one holy Church . . . if we'll let Him.

ACTION SUGGESTIONS

1. Do a group assessment of corporate sin that may exist in your church. Corporately, which attitudes does your church hold that are sinful, or come close to being sinful?

2. Make a list of qualities that describe a Christlike person. Then list at least one person in your local church who, in your opinion, best represents those qualities today, as a living example of Christlikeness. What quality of Christlikeness do you represent to others in your church? This may be helpful to do in smaller groups, such as the church board, your Sunday school class, or any group of people who know and trust one another.

3. Take some "pondering time" to do an assessment of the quality of the means of grace evidenced in your own church. List what you believe to be your church's primary corporate means of grace (from the list in this chapter and by adding others). Rate each of them from one to ten. Which are the strongest "channels" of grace in your church, and which need attention and upgrading?

4. Make a "corporate to-do list" for your church. What are the tiny steps your church, collectively, should take to begin seeking holiness? What may need to change about your preaching, worship, altar services, etc. to help move the church in this direction? Pray about these steps, by yourself, and with others, if possible. Ask yourself, Should we begin to take these steps as a family of Wesleyan believers?

FOR FURTHER READING

Augustine, St. *Homilies on the Gospel of John, Homilies on the First Epistle of John and Soliloquies: Nicene and Post-Nicene Fathers of the Christian Church,* Part 7. Whitefish, Mont.: Kessinger Publishing, 2004.

Benedict of Nursia. *The Rule of St. Benedict*. New York: Vintage Press, 1998.

Bonhoeffer, Dietrich. *Life Together*. New York: HarperSanFrancisco, 1978.

Yoder, John Howard. *Body Politics: Five Practices of the Christian Community Before the Watching World*. Scottdale, Pa.: Herald Press, 2004.

These are among the very best of the vast library available on the subject of Christian holiness in community. All Christian leaders—and pastors, especially—should make themselves acquainted with these classics.

4

The Church Jesus Builds Is
MISSIONAL

J. Michael Fullingim

*Anyone who is joined to Christ is a new being; the old is gone,
the new has come. All this is done by God, who through Christ
changed us from enemies into his friends and gave us the
task of making others his friends also.*

—2 Corinthians 5:17–18 (GNT)

*The Christian Mission is an astonishing phenomenon. A particular move-
ment which began nearly two thousand years ago in a restricted area
of the Middle East has actually gone into all the world. The
penetration of the world by the Gospel of Christ is a direct result
of the fact that Christianity is a missionary faith.*

—Elton Trueblood, *The Validity of the Christian Mission*

I n agreement with Trueblood's triumphant affirmation, the
reader may find it difficult to fathom that only a little over two
hundred years ago the Protestant church paid scant attention to this
matter of bringing the Good News of Christ to the masses of people
in the world who had never heard it.[1] In 1792 William Carey,
deemed the father of modern Protestant missions, found it necessary
to write a pamphlet, entitled *An Enquiry into the Obligation of
Christians to Use Means for the Conversion of the Heathens*, to persuade
his fellow pastors and church leaders in England that being sent out

as a missionary/evangelist was not only theologically appropriate but indeed an obligation of every believer in every church fellowship.

Today it is hard to imagine anyone in the visible church who does not have at least a cursory acquaintance with the missional and apostolic thrust of Matthew 28:18–20, not to mention the whole of the New Testament. Some may argue that in the immediate context of this seminal text, Jesus was directing His Great Commission to His eleven disciples merely for that era (Matt. 28:16). However, I have long assumed that this missional mandate is unmistakably directed to each and every believer to *make disciples* wherever *we* as believers go in this world—regardless of language or cultural barriers encountered. Therefore, when, a few years ago, I was participating in a Sunday school class of a mainline church where I had been invited to speak, I was rather stunned when the teacher of the class seriously challenged my long-held assumption with her well-intentioned comment: "It is presumptuous and imperialistic for an American Christian to assert that his or her religion is superior to other equally valid religions in the world." Somehow— perhaps through her life experience or through the press of *our* culture, or even both—she had become convinced that evangelism in any shape or form was an act of hostility to the very existence of a culture, instead of a joyous occasion of God's love entering in to redeem a people within their culture. I intentionally did not catch her gaze as I delivered my "missionary" message during the morning worship hour—my message being that the Great Commission is neither permission to start a holy war nor warrant for regarding ourselves as superior to others. On the contrary, it makes us their servants!

In light of our increasingly secular culture in North America and the growing hostility in our pluralistic world to the truth claims of the gospel of Christ, what really is the function and purpose of the Church? Has the Church merely become a country club for folks who cannot afford one? God forbid! As one who has dedicated his life to making disciples globally—through personally communicating the gospel in linguistically and culturally relevant ways in diverse settings, as well as training other believers in this missional endeavor—I am convinced the Church Jesus builds is evangelistic and apostolic at its very core. No believer who has personally been redeemed and reconciled by the God of creation through the resurrected Christ is exempt from sharing his or her story of a transformed life with others who live their lives estranged from God.

A MISSIONAL FOCUS UNDERLIES THE OLD TESTAMENT

That the Old Testament conveys a clear missional focus became a matter of debate among scholars in the twentieth century. Without wading unnecessarily through that debate, suffice it to say that the God of the Old Testament was a missional God—whether or not the people of Israel acted on or even believed that they had a responsibility to the nations who were not in a covenant relationship with Yahweh. My assertion is borne out primarily through two prominent Old Testament ideas: *blessing* (e.g., Gen 12:1–3; 26:2–5) and *kingdom of priests* (e.g., Exod. 19:3–6).

Having taught Old Testament Literature at a Wesleyan university for a number of years, I have heard the following lament from several international students taking the course: "It doesn't seem fair that God chose to establish His everlasting covenant with Abraham and his promised descendants." In response to them, I have shared my deeply held conviction that God's call and covenant oath with Abraham entailed not only a personal *blessing* ("I will make you into a great nation and I will bless you; I will make your name great, and you will be a blessing," Gen. 12:2), but also a serious *responsibility* for Abraham and his descendants ("And all peoples on earth will be blessed *through* you," Gen. 12:3, emphasis added). The exact nature of *how* "all peoples on earth" were to be blessed does seem, however, to have remained somewhat of a mystery throughout the Torah, the Prophets, and the Writings—especially without reflection from a New Testament perspective.

Abraham was called out of his polytheistic cultural milieu back to the ethical monotheism of his ancient ancestors, through faithful, covenant obedience to the righteous Lord Almighty. This was the "message" Abraham and his descendants were to convey to all nations, in their role as a priestly nation (Exod. 19:3–6), as mediators with Yahweh on behalf of other people groups outside this covenant relationship.

Lest anyone think this writer is reading into the Abrahamic covenant a theological basis for the missional focus in the Old Testament, it is crucial to note that Peter himself declared this same perspective to the crowd that had gathered on Solomon's Porch in the Temple, when he had healed the crippled beggar shortly after the Day of Pentecost, the very birthday of the Church. Peter said, "And you are heirs of the prophets and of the covenant God made with your fathers. He said to Abraham, 'Through your offspring all peoples on earth will be blessed.' When God raised up his servant, he sent him first to you to bless you by turning each of you from your wicked ways" (Acts 3:25–26). Not surprisingly, the Great Commission is an overarching impetus in the Old Testament!

THE MISSIONAL MANDATE RESTS UPON EVERY TRUE BELIEVER

When Jesus left this world, He gave His followers *one* task and *only* one, "Go and *make disciples of all nations*, baptizing them in the name of the Father and of the Son and of the Holy Spirit, and teaching them to obey everything I have commanded you" (Matt. 28:19–20, emphasis added). Indeed, this has been God's plan for the

peoples of this world since the very beginning. We see this truth articulated even in Simeon's blessing as he holds the infant Messiah in his
arms at the Temple in Jerusalem:

> Lord, now You are letting Your servant depart in peace,
> According to Your word; For my eyes have seen Your salvation
> Which You have prepared *before the face of all peoples, A light
> to bring revelation to the Gentiles* [Gr., *ethnon*], And the glory
> of Your people Israel (Luke 2:29–32, NKJV, emphasis added).

Years later in the city of Damascus, the Lord spoke to a disciple
named Ananias in a vision, instructing him to go to a certain house in
his city and to place his hands on a guest in distress, Saul of Tarsus,
so that Saul's physical eyesight might be restored. Because of Saul's
reputation as a persecutor of the followers of the Way, Ananias strug-
gled with the directive in this vision, until the Lord reassured him
with this message for Saul, "This man is my chosen instrument to
carry my name before the Gentiles and their kings and before the
people of Israel. I will show him how much he must suffer for my
name" (Acts 9:15–16). Saul, later to be called Paul, definitely understood this apostolic mandate given to him to carry the redeeming
name of the resurrected Jesus as Messiah and Lord to the Gentile
world as well as to his fellow Jews. The New Testament record bears
witness that Paul was faithful in fulfilling this obligation "both to
Greeks and non-Greeks." Indeed, Paul declared unabashedly that he
was "not ashamed of the gospel, because it is the power of God for
the salvation of everyone who believes: first for the Jew, then for the
Gentile" (Rom. 1:14, 16, emphasis added).

In his second letter to the Christians at Corinth, Paul affirmed,
"Anyone who is joined to Christ is a new being; the old is gone, the
new has come." He then declared with confidence, "All this is done by

God, who through Christ changed us from enemies into his friends and gave us the task of making others his friends also. Our message is that God was making all human beings his friends through Christ. God did not keep an account of their sins, and he has given us the message which tells how he makes them his friends" (2 Cor. 5:17–19, GNT). God is clearly the one who transforms anyone who is joined to Christ from being an enemy into His friend, and it is equally clear that *anyone* and *every one of us* who has experienced this transformed life has been given the task of instructing and encouraging others to become His friends also. Not one of us is exempt from this missional task.

GOD IS A MISSIONAL GOD

That God wills the salvation of the peoples of the world, then, is unarguably a truth claim of the gospel (2 Pet. 3:8–9). But how can people be joined to Christ when they have never heard of Him? Paul asked this same rhetorical question in his letter to the Christians in Rome:

If you confess with your mouth, "Jesus is Lord," and believe in your heart that God raised him from the dead, you will be saved . . . As the Scripture says, "Anyone who trusts in him will never be put to shame." For there is no difference between Jew and Gentile—the same Lord is Lord of all and richly blesses all who call on him, for, "Everyone who calls on the name of the Lord will be saved." How, then, can they call on the one they have not believed in? And how can they believe in the one of whom they have not heard? And how can they hear without someone preaching to them? And how can they preach unless they are sent? (Rom. 10:9, 11–15).

By posing this series of rhetorical questions, Paul was not inviting dialogue about the missional mandate. Rather, he was using this common literary device to state the obvious: someone must be sent to preach about Jesus if those who have never heard of Him are to hear the good news. Logically, it is only after people hear about Jesus that they can believe in Him. Finally, it is only after people believe in Jesus that they can call on His name for salvation.

This cause-effect chain of events is first set in motion by believers *being sent* (in Greek, *apostalôsin*)—etymologically and semantically connected to the English word *apostle*—meaning "one who is sent"). Paul's use of the passive voice in this clause (Rom. 10:15) allows the sender to remain implicit or otherwise anonymous. In our day, we are familiar with the church being the sender of evangelistic teams into the local community, of short-term mission teams, and even of career missionaries, who are funded through faith-promise giving by individuals and congregations. However, I sense from Paul's writing style that he often uses the passive voice where God himself is the implied agent. To be certain, it is He who is the Lord of the plentiful harvest, but sadly, the workers are few. The instruction follows, "Ask the Lord of the harvest, therefore, to send out workers into his harvest field" (Luke 10:2).

So why is it that workers are still few in our day? The reason can be none other than that we believers are refusing to look beyond our comfortable and safe existence within the church and out at the harvest. Such refusal to be personally involved in the sowing and reaping of the harvest—either through explicit denial or apathetic ignorance of the missional mandate—is clearly opposed to the will of our missional God.

Jesus quite aptly addressed such apathy regarding the business of the kingdom of God in His parable of the talents, recorded in Matthew 25:14–30. Whenever we as believers understand the redemptive work God is doing in the world and participate with Him in accomplishing His desire for all peoples of our world, we will experience the ultimate in joyful success—being rewarded with God's approval, "Well done, good and faithful servant! . . . Come and share your master's happiness" (Matt. 25:21, 23). What a contrast if we remain apathetic to His missional mandate, burying the "talent" entrusted to us: "And throw that worthless servant outside, into the darkness, where there will be weeping and gnashing of teeth" (Matt. 25:30).

The Church's mandate was and continues to be evangelism. Emile Brunner once wrote, "The church exists by mission as fire exists by burning."[2] Only as the Church fulfills its missional obligation to the whole world does it justify its existence. It is only when this most important work of the Church is given to *everyone* in the Church that the Church will indeed demonstrate a vibrant missional focus. Every local church, therefore, must project itself in some vital manner into the whole world through the consistent and integral involvement of each individual believer. Churches should not be measured by *seating* capacity, but rather by *seeding* capacity!

A narrow, inward focus—one that limits ministry and mission to one's own comfort zone of culture and language—will inevitably cause the Church to shirk its responsibility to participate with God in His redemptive concern for all the ethno-linguistic groups of the world. When the members of a local church focus their programs and activities exclusively on themselves to meet their own needs, they demonstrate quite profoundly their apathy and their contentment to leave others in their spiritual darkness. The words "Jesus is the light of the world" are simply words, unless they are proclaimed and tested in the culture and language of the myriad people groups who inhabit our local communities *and* beyond.

As Christians we know that significance, fulfillment, and ultimate success are found only in accomplishing God's will and purpose for our lives—contrary to how our culture defines success. Because God is a missional God, our significance in life can be found only in participating in His global cause. For every believer, there is no greater cause in which to be involved than world evangelization. A local church that actively encourages, challenges, and facilitates practical ways for each believer to develop an outward, missional focus will be fulfilling its function and purpose in developing spiritually alive, "world Christians."

A MISSIONAL CHURCH ESPOUSES A KINGDOM PERSPECTIVE

The Church Jesus builds will be blessed with a *Kingdom perspective* on peoples of every ethnicity and language—regardless of whether they live in the local community or in a far-away place. Such a perspective removes the distasteful distinction between "us" and "them." This is not to say that cultural and language differences are not real; indeed, they are! Rather, it means that in Christ "there is neither Jew nor Greek, slave nor free, male nor female, for *you are all one* in Christ Jesus" (Gal. 3:28, emphasis added).

Peter was the first among the apostles to experience this broadened social horizon, but *only after* the Holy Spirit spurred him on to this missional focus in the house of an unclean Roman soldier. Peter finally got it, evidenced by his statement, "*I now realize* how true it is that God does not show favoritism" (Acts 10:34, emphasis added). The entire thrust of Acts 10 is about the Kingdom perspective that God desires for all who worship Him, a perspective gained only through an intentional focus beyond the narrow confines of one's own language and socio-religious culture.

It is not clear from the record in the book of Acts how much time transpired between that memorable night in Gethsemane when Peter lopped off the ear of a servant who, by his name, may have been a Gentile, perhaps even Roman, and the later events recorded in Acts 10. I wonder what Peter must have been thinking when these three Gentile men—two servants and one *Roman* soldier—came to the gate and told him they had come from Cornelius, a Roman centurion. Could Peter have heard correctly, that this presumably pagan centurion was actually "a righteous and God-fearing man"? Certainly, Peter's cultural rules of social and religious apartheid were soon challenged to the core (Acts 10:28–29).

What were Peter's internal struggles during that two-day, thirty-five mile walk up the seacoast to the city of Caesarea? And how did he, the "brothers from Joppa," and the three Gentiles walk along? In one big, happy, fellowshipping group? Or in two smaller clusters — the three Gentiles up ahead, leading the way, and the small band of Jewish believers following along, perhaps even keeping their distance? The record is silent on the social dynamics of their journey. Nevertheless, regardless of what this group of Jews and Gentiles thought, and how they talked (or didn't talk), we know Peter's own narrow understanding of the Kingdom underwent a profound broadening by the Holy Spirit as he placed one foot in front of the other.

This enhancement of Peter's perspective on the Kingdom started with his mystifying vision of a sheet filled with a host of unclean animals that was let down from heaven to earth, with the strange command, "Kill and eat!" It resulted in his stunning declaration inside the house of an "unclean" Roman centurion, "I now realize how true it is that God does not show favoritism but accepts [people] from *every* nation who fear him and do what is right. You know the message God sent to the people of Israel, telling the good news of peace through Jesus Christ, who is Lord *of all*. . . . All the prophets testify about him that *everyone* who believes in him receives forgiveness of sins through his name" (Acts 10:34–36, 43, emphasis added).

When Peter later explained this incident to his fellow Jewish believers in the Jerusalem church, he said, "As I began to speak, the Holy Spirit came on *them* as he had come on *us* at the beginning. Then I remembered what the Lord had said: 'John baptized with water, but you will be baptized with the Holy Spirit.' So if God gave *them* the same gift as he gave *us*, who believed in the Lord Jesus Christ, who was I to think that I could oppose God?" (Acts 11:15–17, emphasis added). This is truly the Kingdom perspective, and that is what a missional focus espouses: a local church that constantly strives to view others who are culturally and linguistically different *just* as God views them. Our ethnically and politically fragmented world desperately awaits such outwardly focused Christians as active participants in healthy local churches.

THE MISSIONAL FOCUS OF THE NORTH AMERICAN CHURCH MAY BE FOUND WANTING

In his book *Let the Nations Be Glad*, John Piper's emphasis on the centrality of worship is both accurate and commendable. He states, "Missions exists because worship doesn't," with the corollary insight that worship is both the *fuel* of mission and the *goal* of mission.[3] These days, a naive observer might be inclined to believe that the missional focus of local churches must be exploding because so many churches have been working quite diligently "to get the worship right"; simply witness the often heated discussions concerning contemporary worship, traditional worship, blended worship, etc. But why is it a fact that there is no church growth in North America despite the emergence of numerous mega-churches in the past two decades? We are building larger and larger worship centers for ourselves and dedicating them to the God who specifically said He does not dwell in a temple made with hands.

When the church does not maintain its missional purpose, the logical end of such worship centers may be foreshadowed when visiting some of the magnificent cathedrals and church edifices in Europe and Russia. Many of these required hundreds of years to build, yet today many are largely devoid of worshipers and stand primarily as museums and fine examples of medieval and renaissance architecture. With the millions of dollars being spent on our own magnificent centers of worship, it is rather sobering to realize that "the typical church in the USA spends just two percent of its budget on local evangelism, . . . [and, at best,] the picture for overseas efforts is mixed."[4] As for evangelical churches, who are reputed to be more committed to the work of God *in the world*, their "giving rate stands at 2.6 percent to charities of all kinds, not just to churches or missions agencies."[5] More specifically, the local churches of The Wesleyan Church of North America are allocating less than four percent of total church giving to global missions—to those strategic efforts designed for taking the gospel into the "Samarias" and the "uttermost parts" of our world. Consequently, as ninety-six percent of local church monies are being spent in our "Jerusalem" and "Judea," one can only wonder how out of tune we are with the heartbeat and desire of God for the unreached people groups of our world.

Having recently returned from a trip to the Indian subcontinent where my fellow team members and I intentionally met with and interviewed Christians who had been persecuted for their faith, my understanding of evangelism has been deeply challenged and, as a result, enhanced. How ironic it is that in our own nation we have the privilege and right to speak out about our faith in Jesus Christ, but more often than not we choose not to; whereas I have just fellowshipped with believers who have refused to stay silent, where it is not only illegal to share one's faith in Jesus, but where converting to Christianity spells unspeakable persecutions, and where baptizing another person into the faith will end in certain death if caught. Nevertheless, they boldly choose to be missional anyway! One pastor, who had recently been severely beaten by radical Muslims and was still recovering from his injuries, shared with us how he considered it a great joy to suffer for Christ. Speaking with firm conviction, he said, "I will not stop sharing my faith in Jesus with Muslims. I count it a joy to suffer for Him. He is my Lord, and He suffered for me!" Such conviction resonates with the missional and apostolic call, "Go! I am sending you out like lambs among wolves" (Luke 10:3), and it seriously challenges our safe and comfortable Christianity in North America.

I believe in the primacy of the local church in world evangelization. The local church is God's biblically ordained instrument for the witness of His people to a culturally and linguistically diverse world that is alienated from Him. Because of the increasing numbers of culturally diverse people groups in North America, practical, realistic steps for initiating and increasing the missional focus of a local church can be taken nearly immediately, right within their own community or within neighboring communities, as well as beyond, as almost daily the world grows smaller and more accessible through a host of technologies. May our "food" be "to do the will of him who sent [us] and to finish his work." Let us "open [our] eyes and look at the fields! They are ripe for harvest" (John 4:34–35).

ACTION SUGGESTIONS

1. Identify at least three texts from the Old Testament and three from the New Testament that have impacted you regarding the desire of God for all of the nations to know Him. Within the next six months, develop several different sermons from these biblical texts, incorporating new and fresh insights you have gained.

2. Study Acts 10:1 — 11:18, reflecting on how this experience required Jesus' Jewish followers to traverse an enormous *cultural distance* (foreshadowed in Jesus' mandate of Acts 1:8). Helpful hints: Use variously colored pencils to identify different types of information, cultural features, rules, taboos, and other clues to the *cultural distance* that the principal participants in this story had to traverse to fulfill Jesus' instructions in Matthew 28:18–20 and Acts 1:8.

Create several statements of principle or insight that will help you and your church adopt a missional focus on unbelievers outside your own culture or language group.

For each principle or insight you have articulated, develop a corresponding series of practical plans of action to incorporate these truths into your personal life, the individual lives of members of the congregation, and the corporate life of your local church.

3. Research the demographic makeup (ethnic and cultural) of your township or city. You should be able to find information online or at your local library. Begin to think of ways to expand the social and cultural horizons of your church through your own pursuit of meaningful intercultural ministry opportunities.

4. Together with your church leaders, begin to explore practical ways to build significant trust relationships and spiritual friendships with people from other cultural backgrounds and to establish meaningful platforms of ministry to those who are unchurched. Determine a starting date and create a timeline for measuring progress. (If your church ministers in a predominantly homogeneous community, your challenge will be to develop a missional focus through *intentional* experiences. Sermons alone will not do this.)

FOR FURTHER READING

Hunter, George G. *How to Reach Secular People*. Nashville: Abingdon Press, 1992.

This book provides an eye-opening summary of the six watershed events that have precipitated the secularization of the West. Hunter also presents an insightful composite profile of the beliefs, attitudes, and doubts of the typical secular person in the United States. Even more helpful is his exploration of how some believers and churches are effectively reaching secular people.

Hybels, Bill and **Mittelberg**, Mark. *Becoming a Contagious Christian*. Grand Rapids, Mich.: Zondervan Publishing House, 1994.

The authors identify three prerequisites for effective evangelism: high potency, close proximity, and clear communication. They aim to convince the reader that living an authentic, compassionate, sacrificial Christian life in the midst of relationships intentionally built with irreligious folks, coupled with passion and skill in engaging in spiritual conversation, leads to maximum evangelistic impact.

Lo, Jim. *Intentional Diversity: Creating Cross-Cultural Ministry Relationships in Your Church*. Indianapolis: Wesleyan Publishing House, 2002.

This book addresses the need for believers to become intentional in building relationships with the men, women, and children of non-dominant populations in our local communities. The author offers a clear rationale and non-threatening advice for helping your congregation bridge its cultural gaps: learning to appreciate rather than fear the differences in other cultures, understanding the difference between tolerance and compromise, learning how to be culturally sensitive, and finding ways to involve your church in cross-cultural ministry.

Mayers, Marvin K. *Christianity Confronts Culture: A Strategy for Crosscultural Evangelism*. Grand Rapids, Mich.: Zondervan Publishing House, 1987 [1974].

Intercultural ministry is understood as any ministry in which one interacts with people who have grown up learning values and lifestyle patterns different from one's own. Mayers presents principles of intercultural communication within the framework of four models: the importance of trust in intercultural relationships; the cross-cultural understanding of norms and social structures; tools that establish the validity of distinct societies; and illustrations of effective intercultural ministry.

McLaren, Brian D. *More Ready Than You Realize: Evangelism as Dance in the Postmodern Matrix.* Grand Rapids, Mich.: Zondervan Publishing House, 2002.

This book was my first introduction to evangelism specifically addressed to our postmodern milieu. It has more than resonated with students in my evangelism classes at Oklahoma Wesleyan University because McLaren's emphasis on developing "spiritual friendships" is within their reach. McLaren uses the form of a series of e-mail interactions between the author and "Alice," through which he helps us "read between the lines" of this young woman's journey to faith, explaining how he helped fan the embers of her faith into full flame. This book is loaded with insights and principles for evangelism in *any* context.

NOTES

1. This is not to assert or imply there was no missional focus or outreach prior to the two previous two centuries; quite the contrary! The history of the Church is indeed a missional history. See Ruth A. Tucker, *From Jerusalem to Irian Jaya: A Biographical History of Christian Missions,* 2nd ed. (Grand Rapids, Mich. Zondervan, 2004).

2. Emil Brunner, *The Word in the World* (London: Student Christian Movement Press, 1931), 11.

3. John Piper, *Let the Nations Be Glad!—The Supremacy of God in Missions* (Grand Rapids, Mich.: Baker Books, 1993), 11.

4. Stan Guthrie, *Missions in the Third Millennium: 21 Key Trends for the 21st Century* (Waynesboro, Ga.: Paternoster Publishing, 2000), 19.

5. Ibid., 20.

The Church Jesus Builds Is
NURTURING

❋

Roger McKenzie

They devoted themselves to the apostles' teaching and to the fellowship,
to the breaking of bread and the prayers.

—Acts 2:42

If only Christian education were to build its teaching-learning
models around biblical examples from the ministry of Jesus Christ
and biblical teachings about the church as a community, effective
learning would be much more likely to result.

—Ted Ward, *Introducing Christian Education*

W hen people think about the teaching ministry of the
Church, often they think of Sunday school, and seldom little more. The Church's teaching is much more than Sunday school,
which only dates back to about 1780, while the teaching ministry of
the church has been an integral part of its ministry since Jesus
launched it. The Church teaches through evangelistic outreach, small
group ministries, mentoring, catechism, children's church, choirs and
music groups, worship and preaching, Sunday school, and many
more ways. Together, let's examine biblical and theological foundations for the Church's teaching ministry, methodologies employed by
Jesus, and suggestions for making the Church's teaching ministry
stronger for the twenty-first century.

THEOLOGICAL FOUNDATIONS

Jesus' example as a teacher, along with the examples of Old Testament prophets and New Testament apostles, provides a solid foundation of biblical support for the vital ministry of teaching. In grace and compassion, God the Father sent Jesus, God incarnate, among humanity. Jesus then instructed His followers to go among hurting people, to change lives with both God's truth and the compassionate touch of their hands. Further, Jesus' eschatological vision for reconciliation with God and a better future for humanity compelled both Him and His followers to teach.

JESUS' COMMAND TO TEACH

The teaching ministry of the Church grows from the example and commands of Jesus, has its foundations in biblical theology, and is methodologically rooted in the social sciences. The Church teaches as an act of obedience to Christ and in response to the example Jesus set. Christ clearly commanded that His followers teach, when He said in His Great Commission:

All authority in heaven and on earth has been given to me. Go therefore and make disciples of all nations, baptizing them in the name of the Father and of the Son and of the Holy Spirit, and teaching them to obey everything that I have commanded you. And remember, I am with you always, to the end of the age (Matt. 28:18–20, NRSV).

The primary objective in this passage is disciple-making. Jesus mandated teaching both a curricular content that included "everything that I have commanded you," and a lifestyle outcome characterized by obedience (verse 20). Jesus also prescribed that His followers approach teaching as a ministry of presence as they went out among people of all nations.

THE INCARNATION

The Church Jesus builds communicates its message intentionally and personally. The personal touch God employed in the Incarnation is more than just a method among methods. Human touch is vitally important in the church's educational ministry. Nothing can replace the face-to-face meetings of learners with mature Christian teachers.

In the Incarnation, Jesus came and lived among people to give of himself sacrificially and to teach them a better way to live. Jesus taught in obedience to the Father and out of love and compassion for people. Those same concerns should continue to motivate the twenty-first century church's teaching. Jesus came so people could experience abundant life (John 10:10); that includes meaningful living by participation in God's kingdom through mature discipleship and the assurance of eternal life in heaven.

Much of first-century formal Jewish religious practice had become so legalistic that ordinary people found it impossible to live out the dictates of the Pharisees and other religious leaders. Jesus taught that it was not the letter of religious teachers' legalisms, but the intent of their hearts, that justified people before God. Jesus' most stinging indictment of these first-century teachers is recorded in Matthew 23. He charged them with failing to practice what they taught (verse 3)—with making the loads of ordinary folk heavy by their teachings, but then not lifting a finger to help them (verse 4); with coveting for themselves the honor due to God (verses 5–12); and with going far and wide to make converts, only to corrupt them later (verse 15).

Jesus' approach to teaching was quite different. Matthew 9:35–36 describes some of those differences:

Then Jesus went about all the cities and villages, teaching in their synagogues, and proclaiming the good news of the kingdom, and curing every disease and every sickness. When he saw the crowds, he had compassion for them, because they were harassed and helpless, like sheep without a shepherd (Matt. 9:35–36, NRSV).

Jesus came and lived among the people and interacted with them. Matthew, writing that Jesus "saw the crowds," suggests these interactions sensitized Jesus to their needs and that He tailored His teaching to them. Further, when Jesus saw their hurts, he always responded with compassion, resulting in Him ministering to both their spiritual and physical needs. The teacher as shepherd is an important model that emerges from this passage. Shepherding teachers are personally involved in the lives of their learners, nurture and care for them, create a safe environment for learning, and help those learners grow in maturity.

In the verses that follow Matthew's description of Jesus' teaching approach, Jesus told His disciples they were to ask that laborers be sent into the world. Jesus then used those same disciples to answer this prayer when He sent them out (Matt. 9:38—10:1). He sent them to begin engaging in His kind of teaching ministry, to which the Church continues to be called. As a model for the Church's teaching ministry, the Incarnation intertwines the theological and methodological foundations for teaching. Jesus focused on more than content; the fact that He came as a servant communicates much about what God values as foundational in teaching.

ESCHATOLOGY

The kingdom of God, or kingdom of heaven as Matthew preferred to describe it, was central in Jesus' teaching. Jesus' eschatological vision provided for a present-future orientation in the Church's teaching, influencing both its content and its values. The eschatological focus brings hopefulness to the Church's teaching in anticipation of the culmination of human history.

Jesus clearly described many of the central concerns of His kingdom when He announced the beginning of His ministry:

> The Spirit of the Lord is upon me, because he has anointed me to bring good news to the poor. He has sent me to proclaim release to the captives and recovery of sight to the blind, to let the oppressed go free, to proclaim the year of the Lord's favor (Luke 4:18–19, NRSV).

Jesus' words recorded in the Matthew 25 description of the judgment echo these same foundational Kingdom values. The Church's teaching ministry must focus on this emerging Kingdom and develop disciples who will live out these values, which communicate good news in and to a hurting world.

The message of the Kingdom may be one of the emphases in Jesus' teaching that is most overlooked by the contemporary Church. It is easier to count conversions and measure personal holiness issues related to lifestyle than to equip disciples who can effectively engage the complex hurts in the world. The Church Jesus builds will focus its teaching ministry on both calling people to transformed lives and engaging a hurting world.

MATURE DISCIPLESHIP

The teaching ministry of the Church as described and modeled by Jesus involves disciple-making, baptism, and other rites of passage, with the goal of helping people become mature disciples, obedient to the life-changing Word of God. When Jesus encountered potential disciples, His challenge to them was a simple: "Come, follow me." This simple act of following Jesus in obedience minimized the possibility of a person taking on the identity of a disciple without the appropriate commitment.

Conversion is an essential early step in spiritual growth, but conversion is not the primary objective. When the teaching ministry of the church allows conversion to be divorced from the life of discipleship, the result is persons who are, at best, nominal Christians whose participation with Christ and His Church is motivated more by the question, "What's in it for me?" than by the lordship of Christ. Those who claim the name of Christ but have not followed Jesus in discipleship are in a precarious situation. Dietrich Bonhoeffer wrote, "Christianity without discipleship is always Christianity without Christ."[1]

METHODOLOGY FOR THE CHURCH'S TEACHING

Jesus' life and ministry provide valuable methodological insights for teaching. Too much of the contemporary Church's educational ministry has been based on formal schooling models of education. Jesus generally did not teach in classrooms at specified times, utilize printed materials (beyond the Scriptures), or adopt a "one-size-fits-all" kind of curriculum. Despite Jesus' avoidance of these methods that have become overly important for us, He managed to change the direction of the world through His life and teachings.

CONTEXT

Jesus demonstrated a profound understanding of His context, and His teaching engaged the first-century culture (and its subcultures) in creative ways. Jesus' encounter with the woman at the well in John 4 is an example. That Jesus took His followers through Samaria, engaged a Samaritan woman in conversation, and stayed in Sychar as a guest for two days, went against the dominant Jewish religious and social conventions of the day. While our treatments of this passage rightly have focused on Jesus' interactions with the woman, too often we have overlooked what Jesus intended to teach His disciples by choosing to go through Samaria. By this act and many others, Jesus demonstrated to His disciples the depth of His love and concern for all humanity. Further, by going to Samaria, He made it clear that those who followed Him would engage in a teaching ministry with peoples of all cultures.

COMPASSION

When Jesus taught those who had been marginalized by the world, He communicated consolation in His teaching with His words and presence. While ministering with compassion, Jesus led the marginalized to truth. Frequently, after ministering to persons with physical needs, Jesus instructed them to leave their lives of sin. Jesus' healing of the blind man in John 9 is illuminating in at least a couple of ways. First, Jesus directed the blame people received for their maladies away from them. In response to the disciples' question about who was to blame for this man's blindness, Jesus responded that neither he nor his parents were to blame. Second, Jesus demonstrated God's compassion by healing this man on the Sabbath (John 9:14). The idea that keeping the Sabbath was more important than restoring a person to wholeness, the position of many Pharisees, was repugnant to Jesus.

COMMITMENT

As Jesus taught the devout, He led them toward deeper meanings. Many of these would become the teachers who would minister in His name. Jesus would entrust to them His message for the world. His challenge to James and John was to not be so worried about position and recognition (Matt. 20). Jesus urged Nicodemus, a leading teacher in Israel, to recognize and embrace spiritual truths he had trouble seeing, possibly because of his preconceived notions (John 3). In His Sermon on the Mount, Jesus directed His hearers to deeper meanings when He repeatedly said, "You have heard that it was said . . . but I tell you" (Matt. 5:21–22, 27–28, 33–34, 38–39, 43–44).

However, to those who were superficially religious, Jesus brought significant challenge. The rich young ruler, though claiming an exemplary religious life, had more of a superficial than a substantive commitment to God. Jesus was patient in listening to his story and discerning his need. When it was time to call him to commitment, as recorded in Luke 18, Jesus challenged the superficial nature of his relationship with God and called the young man to a significant change in his affections and lifestyle by embracing Him as Lord and giving sacrificially to the poor.

COMMUNICATION

As an itinerant teacher, Jesus communicated very well. However, Jesus did not limit His methods to lecturing and preaching. As He taught, Jesus used a wide-ranging variety of methods to structure learning that got people's attention, created memorable, life-shaping experiences, and connected with their lives on multiple levels.

Because Jesus chose to do His teaching outside the classroom, He avoided predictability. Jesus so thoroughly integrated His life and ministry that He was able to seize "teachable moments" as they walked along the way. The disciples learned to relate to one another as Jesus modeled ministry and as they engaged in ministry.

Part of what made Jesus such an effective teacher was that He communicated in extraordinarily memorable ways. Expounding on propositions was not nearly as prominent in Jesus' teaching as storytelling. Jesus addressed profound truths in stories that were well-crafted and memorable. As people recalled and retold His stories, they reconnected to those profound meanings. Embedded in Jesus' stories about ordinary people, places, and happenings were deep layers of truth.

COMMEMORATIONS

Milestones and commemorations were focal points of Jesus' ministry. It was at the wedding in Cana that Jesus performed His first miracle. Not only did Jesus participate in these events, but as a teacher He also gave new meanings to existing celebrations and created rites of passage. Jesus had to insist on it before John would baptize Him; later, Jesus commanded His followers to baptize initiates into the Church. At His final Passover meal celebration, Jesus began the tradition of the Lord's Supper by utilizing the ordinary elements of that meal. These milestones and commemorations continue to instruct Jesus' followers and communicate grace and truth to those who participate in them.

Jesus' teaching effected change in people's lives because He touched their intellect, emotions, and life choices at the points of their interests and needs. Many churches have fallen into the trap of focusing too much on only one domain of learning. Some churches primarily address people's intellect. Other churches tend to major on emotions. Still others are caught up almost entirely in what people do. People think, they feel, and they do, so when the church's teaching ministry does not address all three of these learning domains, it is difficult for people to comprehend, value, and act on truth.

Holistic living was central to Jesus' teaching and concerns. Jesus was particularly harsh in His indictments of religious leaders of His time because they failed to integrate their religious life with their everyday life. James captured Jesus' concern when he wrote that followers of Jesus were to "be doers of the word, and not merely hearers who deceive themselves" (James 1:22, NRSV). The church Jesus builds will not just communicate content for the sake of knowledge, but will call people to a transformation that both beckons and enables them to live out the Kingdom values of the Lord.

APPLICATION IN THE CONTEMPORARY CHURCH

Emphasizing mature discipleship as a primary objective of the church's ministry, rather than focusing on particular programs, would strengthen the church's discipling ministry and thereby have the potential for greater impact in the world. Over the past several decades, the Sunday school has declined, yet in many contexts it remains viable. However, where Sunday school is not doing well, leaders must explore other approaches for discipling people of all ages. Most churches will need to provide multiple approaches to teaching and disciple-making.

A strategic approach to discipleship is essential to help Christians live fully integrated lives. The following emphases are essential, though not necessarily sequential: First, the church's teaching must stress the transforming power of the gospel; in salvation, Christ transforms, and the maturing Christian continues to be transformed after the likeness of Christ. Second, obedience to God and His Word are critical for people to respond to His call in their lives. Third, a teaching ministry that emphasizes growth and maturation communicates that believers can experience greater holiness and readiness for ministry involvement throughout their lives. Fourth and finally, the church's teaching must equip and engage in Kingdom ministries that involve disciples in transformational ministries in the world.

Some suggest we view these emphases as concentric circles or as bases on a baseball diamond. While those metaphors are helpful on some levels, ultimately they are inadequate, as these teaching foci resist simplistic sequencing.

Thomas Groome's shared praxis teaching approach provides a more adequate model for helping followers toward faithful living in light of Christ's kingdom message. Groome describes the shared praxis approach to teaching "as a group of Christians sharing in dialogue their critical reflection on present action in light of the Christian Story and its Vision toward the end of lived Christian faith."[2] Groome's model includes five steps:

The first step is identifying a present activity that is common to the group. The second step involves critical reflection on that activity by the group and engaging in dialogue about the activity. In the third step, the teacher introduces the Story (including the Scriptures and the church's tradition) as it applies to their activity. Fourth, the teacher invites learners to appropriate the Story to their own lives and to examine their lives in light of the Story. Fifth, group members are challenged to embrace personally a better, truer vision of the kingdom of God that grows from the Story, and then are called to live out that vision faithfully.[3]

Much of the value of Groome's shared praxis approach for the church's teaching ministry is that it begins where learners are and then draws them toward more faithful living in response to the Kingdom values of the gospel. This approach can be accomplished largely in the classroom, though it begins outside the classroom and later sends learners out to apply the truths of the gospel in faithful living, in conformity to a clearer vision of the Kingdom message.

CONCLUSION

A teaching ministry that results in learners opening their lives to accountability and faithful living must be built on relationships. Learners need teachers who are physically present, emotionally accessible, and trustworthy. Because teachers are vital to the success of its teaching ministry, the church must focus more on equipping excellent teachers. It is not enough to provide teachers with space and materials. If teachers are to guide learners to a better future, they must be good exegetes of both Scripture and culture. A vital part of the church's educational ministry is the active cultivation of excellent teachers.

John Wesley's ministry illustrates a well-contextualized model of many of Jesus' teaching approaches. Wesley was effective in his preaching and in his use of small group experiences for teaching and discipleship. In fact, Wesley utilized a variety of kinds of small groups to achieve different teaching purposes. Recently, the focus of the church's *teaching* has shifted too much toward the *preaching* in the main worship service and away from the smaller group experiences. For the church to have a truly effective teaching ministry, we must adopt a view of teaching that focuses more on learning for application rather than on transmission of content. Learning for application is much more likely in smaller environments than in the large, congregational forums.

The challenge for the Church in the twenty-first century is great. The example of Jesus and the potential for transformed lives for Kingdom living should motivate the Church to elevate the ministry of teaching to the prominent level Jesus himself gave it throughout His earthly ministry.

ACTION SUGGESTIONS

1. Create a flowchart of your church's teaching ministry plan. Map out the journey from cradle to senior adult through your church's educational ministry. Next, map out the passage from seeking non-Christian to mature Kingdom-engaged disciple. If these journeys are not clear, consider reviewing your church's overall educational ministry plan.

2. Reflect on your personal teaching style; it may be helpful to review some of your recent lesson plans. Remember we are prone to teach as we were taught and to teach to our own primary learning styles. Ask yourself, Am I more likely to teach to learners' intellect (cognition), emotions (affections), or actions (life choices)? As you plan your teaching (and preaching), intentionally construct your objectives and activities to touch all three learning domains.

3. Outline your church's strategies to recruit and equip people to be excellent teachers. What preparation do new teachers get before you "turn them loose" in the classroom? How do you continue to evaluate and support the growth of your teachers?

4. Many churches now involve people of all ages in mission trips. Are your learners growing as much as they could from these experiences? As you plan for your next trip, be intentional about connecting acts of service to the lifestyle of Christ. Make sure you plan for times of reflection on mission trip activities in light of the gospel before, during, and after your experience.

FOR FURTHER READING

Groome, Thomas H. *Christian Religious Education: Sharing Our Story and Vision*. San Francisco: Jossey-Bass, 1999.

Many in the field of Christian education consider Groome's book a classic. He discusses theological, historical, and philosophical foundations for educational ministry and provides concrete approaches to strengthen the church's teaching through shared praxis. Chapter ten, "Shared Praxis in Praxis," is particularly helpful.

Palmer, Parker J. *To Know as We Are Known: A Spirituality of Education*. San Francisco: Harper & Row, 1983.

Palmer's book provides a well-reasoned foundation for viewing education as a spiritual journey. Though this book was not primarily written about the Church's teaching ministry, it includes helpful insights for all who endeavor to teach others.

Richards, Lawrence O. and **Bredfeldt**, Gary J. *Creative Bible Teaching*. Chicago: Moody Press, 1998.

This book is a a very practical resource for teachers. Richards and Bredfeldt take teachers through five steps toward great teaching: studying the Bible, focusing the message, structuring the lesson, teaching the class, and evaluating results. Particularly helpful are the instruction on inductive Bible study and the emphasis on teaching for life change.

NOTES

1. Dietrich Bonhoeffer. *The Cost of Discipleship*, 1st Touchstone ed. (New York: Simon and Schuster, 1995), 59.

2. Thomas H. Groome. *Christian Religious Education: Sharing our Story and Vision* (San Francisco: Harper and Row, 1980), 184.

3. Ibid., 184–201.

The Church Jesus Builds Is

COMPASSIONATE

Donald D. Wood

The Spirit of the Lord is on me, because he has anointed me to preach good news to the poor. He has sent me to proclaim freedom for the prisoners and recovery of sight for the blind, to release the oppressed, to proclaim the year of the Lord's favor.

—Luke 4:18–19

This is the great reason why the providence of God has so mingled you together with other men, that whatever grace you have received of God, may, through you, be communicated to others.

—John Wesley, "The Sermon on the Mount," Discourse IV

TAO OR GOLDEN RULE?

Empathy characterized the life and teaching of Jesus and fulfills both the Law and the Prophets of the Hebrew Scriptures. Compassion reflects the spirit of the church in Acts and the ethical teaching of the New Testament Epistles. Caring has been descriptive of the Church at her best in all ages.

Jesus' manifesto at the beginning of His earthly ministry—His quotation of and affirmation that He is the fulfillment of Isaiah's prophecy—reaches beyond the universal Tao of "do no harm," a characteristic teaching of the world's major religions and philosophical systems. Jesus modeled and taught a more activist principle of initiating mercy and compassion. Later, Jesus gave His followers the Golden Rule, saying, "So in everything, do to others what you would have them do to you, for this sums up the Law and the Prophets" (Matt. 7:12).

The form of the Golden Rule which many have learned is, "Do unto others as you would have them do unto you." Not only Jesus, but also Confucius, Aristotle, Hillel, and Chesterfield laid down this maxim. However, none of the others put it forth quite as altruistically as Jesus; all lean at least a bit toward the negative phrasing of the Tao. The point is, one can obey the Tao by doing nothing, but the Golden Rule, in its dynamic form as proclaimed by Jesus, requires activity. Compassion functions by doing rather than by not doing. It is not isolating, but relational.

CARING IN THE HEBREW SCRIPTURES

Although Genesis describes many dysfunctional families and certain portions of the Mosaic Law strike modern ears as harsh (for example, stoning rebellious children), active mercy appears in the story of Joseph and his brothers. Mercy continues in the Law, which commands compassion. Caring is expected and involves more than altruistic emotions. Among these humane provisions in the Law are the legislative requirements of the Sabbath and Sabbath years, the provisions for the years of Jubilee (though without historical records that show them being practiced), the laws of gleaning, the rights of the daughters of Zelophehad to inherit property when their father died without male heirs, and even giving back a man his cloak for the night if one held it as surety for a loan not yet repaid.

The Sabbath was a weekly reminder not only of God's rest in creation (Exod. 20:11) but also of human rest from the hard labor required by the Egyptians (Deut. 5:15). The Sabbath and Jubilee years mandated canceling debt and freeing slaves. Gleaning was a compassionate program for those who were poor, such as Ruth and Naomi. The daughters of Zelophehad were about to lose their father's inheritance because he had left no male heirs, but Moses took their plea before God and established the principle that women without brothers could inherit land to keep it in the family. Cloaks were not only for dress but also for use as sleeping bags for warmth at night. From such ancient provisions of God's law, the church hears the early call to provide for the less fortunate people in the community.

The post-Mosaic history of the Hebrew Scriptures includes much blood-letting inflicted both on enemies and on fellow Hebrews, but the prophets continued to remind generals and kings they were not exempt from the expectations of mercy found in the Law. Nathan went face-to-face with David about the adultery he committed with Uriah's wife, and Elijah prophesied Ahab and Jezebel's bloody demise for their theft of Naboth's vineyard; the forecasted destinies of each were fulfilled.

Among the writing prophets, calls for compassionate response on behalf of the marginalized reached a crescendo. "'It is you who have ruined my vineyard; the plunder from the poor is in your houses. What do you mean by crushing my people and grinding the faces of the poor?' declares the Lord" (Isa. 3:14–15). When the people asked why God paid little attention to their fasting, Isaiah gave them God's reply:

Is not this the kind of fasting I have chosen: to loose the chains of injustice and untie the cords of the yoke, to set the oppressed free and break every yoke? Is it not to share your food with the hungry and to provide the poor wanderer with shelter—when you see the naked, to clothe him, and not to turn away from your own flesh and blood? (Isa. 58:6–7).

Ezekiel wrote this word against the leaders of his day: "Woe to the shepherds of Israel who only take care of themselves! Should not shepherds take care of the flock? . . . You have not strengthened the weak or healed the sick or bound up the injured. You have not brought back the strays or searched for the lost. You have ruled them harshly and brutally" (Ezek. 34:2, 4).

Amos became downright offensive in his characterization of Samaria's women and their lack of compassion: "Hear this word, you cows of Bashan on Mount Samaria, you women who oppress the poor and crush the needy and say to your husbands, 'Bring us some drinks'" (Amos 4:1). Again, he said, "You trample on the poor and force him to give you grain" (Amos 5:11). Later, Amos addressed this shortage of empathy for the plight of fellow Israelites in these words:

Hear this, you who trample the needy and do away with the poor of the land, saying, "When will the New Moon be over that we may sell grain, and the Sabbath be ended that we may market wheat?"—skimping the measure, boosting the price and cheating with dishonest scales, buying the poor with silver and the needy for a pair of sandals, selling even the sweepings with the wheat (Amos 8:4–6).

To state the issue positively, Micah surely had it right when he wrote, "He has showed you, O man, what is good. And what does the LORD require of you? To act justly and to love mercy and to walk humbly with your God" (Mic. 6:8).

CARING IN THE NEW TESTAMENT

When we turn to the pages of the New Testament, it is clear that the teachings of Jesus—by word and example, and ultimately by His sacrificial death—guide His body, the Church, in the direction of compassionate ministry. Clearly the Hebrew Scriptures taught that God desires mercy more than sacrifice, and that concern for one's neighbors is paramount as an expression of one's worship of the Lord. However, following the Judeans' return from their Babylonian captivity, a scribal tradition arose that replaced the bright sun of compassion with an emphasis on ritual, without much concern for mercy or even for justice. To use a metaphor from Jesus himself, these experts in the Law strained out gnats while swallowing camels. The Pharisees became major players and interpreters of the Law, too often replacing the actual Mosaic Law with a more legalistic form of religion.

When Jesus came, He highlighted the humble widow and her small contribution rather than the wealthy donors' offerings, which they presented with fanfare. Jesus felt the lepers' pain and social isolation; He enjoyed the company of social outcasts; and He had time for children, even when His disciples tried to keep them from bothering Him. He made social outcasts the righteous ones in His stories, and leveled harsh criticism at the supposedly righteous leaders. Women with shadowy pasts were not off limits for Jesus; rather, He gave them bright futures. Others saw people as they were, and asked, "Why?" Jesus' eyes of compassion saw people as who they could become, and He asked, "Why not?"

Jesus' eschatological parables clearly communicate that His values have implications for His future kingdom. They teach that the *then* is the outcome of the *now*. The foundations of both wise and foolish builders in the *now* are crucial to surviving the storms of the *then*. The wheat and the weeds are allowed to continue their growth until the harvest, when the separation occurs. The separation of the good and bad fish comes when the net is emptied. The rich fool's bigger barns and intended ease are worth nothing to him when death calls. The wealthy man's refusal to meet poor Lazarus' need when he had the opportunity to do so has its culmination in his own future fiery demise. All the parables found in Matthew 24 work with this *now* and *then* tension, but it becomes most clear in the separation of the sheep and the goats. Neither those who acted compassionately nor those who failed to act compassionately were aware that Jesus himself stood before them. The eschatological view of the Church taught by Jesus teaches that the future is now. The blessing or condemnation is born, lives, and dies in the present moment in which one acts or fails to act. Jesus has come, is here, and will come in the opportunities for caring that meet us on a regular basis.

Compassionate ministry characterized the life of the early Church as well. The description of Pentecost is followed immediately by the description of the fellowship of the believers: "Selling their possessions and goods, they gave to anyone as he had need" (Acts 2:45). Peter healed a crippled beggar (Acts 3); believers shared their possessions (Acts 4); the church met the needs of Greek-speaking widows (Acts 6); Stephen's last prayer was a request for God to pardon those who were stoning him (Acts 7); and the compassion extended to the Philippian jailer by his Christian inmates opened the way to salvation for him and his family (Acts 16).

The Epistles continue this emphasis on Christlike love, from Romans through the letters of John. The early Church certainly did face serious challenges, and some of those challenges called for decisions to remove from fellowship those who offended the principles of Christ. There is a time for the Church to condemn attitudes and practices that do not reflect fidelity to the lordship of Christ and to judge those who fail to live in love with fellow believers.

However, the overwhelming message of these letters is the good word that has come through the ministry of Christ and the Holy Spirit. The early Church won the respect of the Mediterranean world by its compassion and self-sacrifice, much more than by what it condemned.

Paul's discussion about the weak and the strong in Romans 14 encourages compassion in the Church concerning differences in such "small" matters as diet and special day observances. James 1:27 defines pure religion as looking after orphans and widows, as well as keeping oneself unpolluted.

CARING IN THE HISTORY OF THE CHURCH

Since the close of the New Testament, the stories of the Church most fondly recalled by her members are the moments of self-sacrificing love. The disputes about the person of Christ, the content of the canon of Scripture, the number and function of the sacraments, and the various divisions in the body are not irrelevant; great defenders of the faith such as Athanasius, Augustine, John of Damascus, Anselm, Aquinas, Luther, Calvin, Barth, and Bonhoeffer are not to be forgotten. However, it is the great practitioners of compassion who are most admired both by the world and by the various branches of the Church. People such as St. Francis, John Wesley, and more recently, Nate Saint and Mother Teresa are attractive models of what the Church should be.

The Wesleyan Revival in England was especially noteworthy in the ministries of compassion by Wesley and those influenced by the movement he initiated. Wesley's preaching changed miners and other day laborers and helped them see their worth to God. Methodist societies and class meetings helped bring about spiritual and moral accountability. Wesley's movement influenced Wilberforce to speak out against slavery, Robert Raikes to begin Sunday schools, and Thomas Howard to work for prison reform.

Wesley himself lived and died an Anglican, but the Methodist movement has been marked by the championing of those marginalized by society. Early on in the United States, the Wesleyan Methodists advocated the abolition of slavery and supported the rights of women to vote, to inherit property, and to preach the gospel. In those days, as in ours, a majority of Christians considered such issues outside the mission of the Church, which most viewed as preaching the gospel, but leaving social structures undisturbed. Christian social activism, however, springs from the conviction that preaching the gospel always has consequences in the lives of those who truly hear the Word. Had the Good Samaritan kept finding victims of robbery and assault on the road to Jericho, surely he would have continued to care for them, but may he not also have begun advocating for greater police protection?

An illustration of hearing but not doing the Word is the (perhaps apocryphal) story of a woman attempting to collect money and food for neighbors whose house had burned. After repeatedly hearing others respond to her pleas for assistance for the burned-out family by saying they "felt" sorry for their unfortunate neighbor but had nothing to spare, she told them, "You are not feeling in the right place; you are not feeling in your pocket." A compassionate Christian faith has both an open heart and an open wallet. Paul expected that predominantly Gentile churches not only would pray for the poor of the church in Jerusalem, but also would contribute money for their material welfare, and so they did (see 2 Cor. 9:1–5).

WILL CARING CHARACTERIZE THE CONTEMPORARY CHURCH?

With this biblical and historical overview as her history, what should the compassionate Church be doing today? How can she incarnate the biblical and historical examples mentioned in this chapter into a living word for this generation? Current responses suggest that both individuals and groups that constitute the Church are offering opportunities for service. Serving meals, running errands, and restoring broken hearts represent just some of the everyday work of believers who sound no trumpets. Additionally, the efforts of Christian relief organizations, such as World Hope International and Samaritan's Purse, channel resources to places of need. Believers working in more secular organizations also provide help and hope for those in dire straits. However, the mobilization of a much higher percentage of the visible Church could multiply the number of compassionate incarnations of the Word.

In his book *The Body: Being Light in Darkness*, Charles Colson tells the compelling story of Rusty Woomer as an example of Christ's body becoming incarnate in the contemporary world. Rusty was the son of an alcoholic father who frequently fought his own demons by abusing his family. Rusty's mother took him to church on occasion, but it never affected his life significantly. Drugs, alcohol, and a variety of social dysfunctions marked his younger years. Finally, spaced out on booze and drugs, Rusty raped and murdered two women in South Carolina and landed on death row in the state penitentiary in Columbia.

While Rusty's life spiraled out of control, Bob McAlister lived a life of comfort and privilege. He was regularly in church and was respected in both social and political circles. However, Bob began to long for a closer walk with God and for a larger purpose in his life. Then Bob met Odell. Odell was wheelchair bound, but he regularly looked out for two homebound women. He traveled miles in his wheelchair to get food for them. Touched by the commitment of Odell's care for the two women, Bob began to look for ways to care for others and eventually signed up for volunteer work with Prison Fellowship.

Bob's first encounter with Rusty was on a weekend as Bob walked down Rusty's cellblock. Rusty sat on the floor surrounded by used candy wrappers, pornographic magazines, partially eaten sandwiches, and cockroaches. Bob's first conversation with Rusty was brief, but Bob said something that God used to change both their lives, "Rusty, you need to call on the name of Jesus." Perhaps to Bob's surprise, Rusty did, confessing his sins that same day. Three days later, when Bob came back, the difference in Rusty and his cell was like midnight and noonday. There was Rusty, "clothed and in his right mind." Over the next few years Bob saw his new brother write letters to the families of those he had killed and rejoiced with Rusty when one relative sent back a moving letter of forgiveness. Their friendship continued to the day Rusty died in the electric chair.[1] Where would Bob have been without Odell? And where would Rusty have been without Bob? Was this merely serendipity or was this providence?

BEWARE OF THE BYSTANDER EFFECT

Several decades ago, Kitty Genovese became a nationally recognized figure due to the circumstances of her death. In the early morning of March 13, 1964, she died in the stairwell of her apartment building in the Kew Gardens district of Queens, New York, after being stabbed in the parking lot. Her attacker returned two more times, repeatedly stabbing her. Nearly forty people heard her cries for help and did nothing.

Out of this tragedy, psychologists eventually began to describe the "bystander effect," which predicts that the more people who witness such a tragedy, the less likely it is that any one of them will step forward to become involved. The contagious attitude of "let someone else do it" has a neutralizing effect on bystanders, while the victim suffers the consequences of the bystanders' failure to act on what surely must have stirred their hearts.

Jesus' miracles frequently took place in situations where many witnesses knew of the pain and suffering of troubled and crippled people but did nothing, except perhaps to think, "There, but for the

120

grace of God, go I." Maybe they were paralyzed by the bystander effect; perhaps they felt impotent to bring about change; perhaps they were just busy; or perhaps they were late for an appointment. Whatever the case, Jesus makes clear in His story of the Good Samaritan that the one who was the neighbor was the one whose empathy prompted him to stop, bind up the wounds, provide for future care, and come back to settle the extra charges.

The shortest verse in the English Bible is John 11:35, "Jesus wept." Why did Jesus weep? When He began to cry, bystanders said, "See how he loved him!" (John 11:36). However, Jesus wept not only because He loved Lazarus, but also out of empathy for Mary's tears. As was typical of Jesus, He then moved beyond tears to take an action that was possible for Him: He raised Lazarus from the dead.

What is possible for us? Most likely we will not raise someone from the dead as Jesus did, but tearful empathy may sow seeds of faith, and Hebrews 11:35 assures us that, in some cases, by faith, "women received back their dead, raised to life again." Still, compassion can cause wonderful happenings *for* others and *in* us.

ACTION SUGGESTIONS

1. Read and consider the message of the Old Testament prophets concerning God's commands for justice and fairness for the poor and the stranger.

2. Read the synoptic Gospels, looking for ways Jesus showed His concern for those on the fringes of society.

3. Read Charles Colson and Ellen Santini's *Being the Body,* especially part three.

4. Consider culturally sensitive ways to befriend people of other faiths in your community—not as "targets" or "trophies," but as human beings.

5. Volunteer for one of the relief organizations in your community: Helping Hands, Habitat for Humanity, Prison Fellowship, a soup kitchen, a home for the elderly, an after-school program, etc.

FOR FURTHER READING

Bonhoeffer, Dietrich. *The Cost of Discipleship*. New York: The Macmillan Company, 1960.

This is *the* classic on the meaning and the cost of following the ethics of Jesus.

Colson, Charles and **Vaughn**, Ellen. *Being the Body*. Nashville: Thomas Nelson/W Publishing Group, 2003.

Part three of this book gives some wonderful examples of ways that both bodies of believers and individuals can bring light to dark places.

Issler, Klaus. *Wasting Time with God: A Christian Spirituality of Friendship with God*. Downers Grove, Ill.: InterVarsity Press, 2001.

This is a wonderful little book about experiencing God's presence in all areas of our ordinary lives, including service with and to others.

NOTES

1. Charles Colson, *The Body: Being Light in Darkness* (Dallas: Word Publishing, 1992), 385–409.

The Church Jesus Builds Is

WORSHIPFUL

Robert Black

God is spirit, and his worshipers must worship in spirit and in truth.

—John 4:24

To worship is to quicken the conscience by the holiness of God, to feed the mind with the truth of God, to purge the imagination by the beauty of God, to open the heart to the love of God, to devote the will to the purpose of God.

—William Temple, Archbishop of Canterbury, in a BBC broadcast, 1944

L ast Sunday I worshipped God in the company of other believers. The congregation of which I was a part was a cross section of our community—white and black, young and no-longer-quite-so-young, doctor, lawyer, public school teacher, homemaker, clerk, accountant, social worker, retiree, you name it. We sang together, prayed together, looked into the Word together, and took the Lord's Supper together, much as Christians have been doing for two millennia.

Next Sunday we'll do it again because the Church Jesus builds is a worshipping community.

Jesus modeled that himself. It was in the context of a worship service in His hometown synagogue that He made His most radical statement, proclaiming himself to be the Messiah (Luke 4), and it was in Jerusalem's Temple that He performed His most radical act, cleansing it of its merchandisers and cheats (Mark 11). He healed and taught in those worship centers repeatedly; in fact, almost fifteen percent of the Gospel narrative is set either in the Temple courts or in a synagogue. Even when He was elsewhere, worship—both private and public—was often the subject of His discourses or the point of His parables.

It's not surprising, then, that worship has always been important to His Church as well. The very first description of the very first church focuses on its worship as well as its fellowship and evangelism (Acts 2:42–47), and from their generation to ours the impulse to worship corporately in local congregations of the universal Church has been a constant. From time to time there have been countering trends, like the Jesus People of the 1960s who famously chanted "Jesus, yes—the Church, no," and George Barna's equally famous identification (and endorsement) of millions of twenty-first century Christians who have substituted the "personal 'church' of the individual" for the local church.[1] However, theology trumps trends—heaven help us if it doesn't—and even though evangelicals may sometimes be shaky on ecclesiology, we are not so reckless as to write off the local church when it is so pervasively written into Scripture.

Our rehearsal for corporate worship around the heavenly throne (Rev. 4–5) is corporate worship here on earth, and despite announcements to the contrary, rehearsal has not been cancelled.

ONE LORD, ONE FAITH, MANY WORSHIP STYLES

Granted, the shape worship takes across the Church is anything but uniform. Conventional wisdom tends to contrast traditional and contemporary worship, as if those were the only two categories. Actually, Christians worship in a wide variety of styles.

A WORSHIP SPECTRUM

Four families stand out:

Liturgical worship is rich in design and order, following fixed patterns prescribed in a book of worship like the Roman Catholic missal or the Anglican/Episcopalian *Book of Common Prayer*. Clergy in colorful vestments preside over services typically marked by a holy hush. Those services focus more on the table than on the pulpit, with the Eucharist (the Lord's Supper) observed weekly as the central event of the hour. Written prayers are the norm, multiple Scripture passages are read, and the Christian Year is observed extensively.

In *classical Protestant worship,* the center of gravity shifts from the sacrament to the sermon. The minister, generally robed in a less elaborate Geneva gown, is primarily a preacher of the Word. Communion is not served at every service, though it is still served frequently. Formal litanies and ascriptions are mingled with extemporaneous prayers, the choir may share responsibility with a soloist for providing special music, and a trimmed-down version of the Christian Year guides the calendar of the congregation. In short, the service is less formal than the worship of more liturgical churches but is still carefully structured.

Revivalistic worship is, to a great degree, the product of spiritual movements like the Wesleyan Revival in England and the First and Second Great Awakenings in America, along with the influence of the American frontier. No robes for the clergy here. Marked by less structure and more spontaneity, the service allows for the added dimension of personal witness, through both spoken testimonies and gospel songs. Altar-call evangelism is standard practice, communion is only occasional, and the Christian Year is largely limited to Christmas and Easter.

What is typically called *contemporary worship* is a high-tech, high-energy worship experience with a high level of involvement expected of the worshipers. (It should be noted that "contemporary" is, by definition, a fluid term, and today's "contemporary" may be tomorrow's "retro," almost literally.) Music plays a major role, even more so than in the other worship styles; praise choruses and contemporary Christian songs predominate. In fact, it's not unusual to find the designation "worship" specifically reserved in these churches for the musical portion of the service, led by a worship team and often supplemented by drama and even liturgical dance. The sermon is positive, uplifting, and dynamic. Dress is casual, the chancel is usually pulpit-free, and banks of flexible seating are the new pews.

Those banks of seats are usually filled with worshipers. Contemporary worship has a significant appeal to youth and young adults in particular, and the growth curve has not gone unnoticed. The explosive popularity of contemporary worship in recent years has produced at least two significant results.

WORSHIP RENEWAL OR WORSHIP WARS?

One result is a fresh focus on worship in the Church at large, whatever the form. Half a century ago, A. W. Tozer surveyed evangelicalism with alarm. Worship, he lamented, was the missing jewel of the Church.[2] If he could survey the modern Church, he might reach a different conclusion. He certainly would be amazed to find volumes on worship spilling off the shelves in Christian bookstores, magazines devoted to worship lying on coffee tables alongside *Newsweek* and *TV Guide*, and worship music as a *multi*-multi-million dollar business. Worship-themed conferences consistently pack in the faithful, and the fastest-growing category of ministerial service seems to be worship pastor. To all appearances, evangelicals—and not just those evangelicals who favor contemporary worship—seem to have recovered their jewel. There is certainly a renewed interest in worship.

Unfortunately, renewed interest doesn't always mean worship renewal.

In this case, it all too often means worship *wars*, the second and decidedly less desirable result of the popularity of contemporary worship. Christian soldiers separate into two camps: "traditional," by which is meant, depending on the denomination, any of the first three approaches to worship; and "contemporary." Each camp then proceeds to wage war on the wrong enemy. Forgotten in all of this is Acts 2:42–47, in which worship and fellowship go hand in hand. For worship differences to lead to a breach in fellowship is tragic. The following two real-life examples will stand for the many:

- A worship seminar ended with a question and answer session. When someone asked, "How can we encourage older people to be more open to contemporary worship?" the leader answered, "You have to understand that older people just don't know how to worship."[3]

- The church board member was adamant. "Contemporary worship is contemporary, all right, but it isn't worship. It's contemporary Christian entertainment. That's fine in its place, but its place is not in the church, disguised as a worship service."

WHERE IS GOD ON SUNDAY MORNING?

One starting point in negotiating a truce in the worship wars might be to note that Acts 2:42–47 closes a chapter in which the Holy Spirit filled the believers. Seriously! Another would be to look at the range of worship styles as points on a line rather than as separate rooms, each with its own door locked.

FORM AND FREEDOM

Imagine a line drawn from "form" on the right to "freedom" on the left. The four families of worship styles fit logically on this continuum, moving in progression from the liturgical approach to less structured worship, and the flow is apparent. Design and order move increasingly toward spontaneity, elaboration toward simplicity, common worship (the corporate stress on "we") toward individual worship expression and experience. As the principal activity of the service shifts from sacrament to sermon to personal witness (as in, for example, Old Style Quaker or charismatic worship), the impetus for the service shifts from table to pulpit to pew. Prayers become spontaneous, Scripture lessons are reduced in number, and the frequency of communion observance declines.

The most important question is, "Where is God on that line?" As much as we are tempted to plant the flag on our own space, we know very well that the answer is, "Anywhere He is worshipped in spirit and in truth." Christ defined worship for the Samaritan woman not in terms of its site (Mt. Gerizim versus Jerusalem) or its shape (Samaritan practices versus Jewish practices), but of its center. At the heart of worship is the Truth (John 14:6), Christ himself, whom we worship and in whom we worship. His characterization of genuine worship is both eschatological and incarnational: "A time is coming when you will worship the Father neither on this mountain nor in Jerusalem. . . . A time is coming and has now come when the true worshipers will worship the Father in spirit and truth, for they are the kind of worshipers the Father seeks. God is spirit, and his worshipers must worship in spirit and in truth" (John 4:21, 23–24).

These familiar words often are understood as a prophecy that both the Samaritan and Jewish sanctuaries would be destroyed, but they actually carry much more significance than that. Christ was speaking not so much about the end of one era as the beginning of another, one that would last forever. He was redirecting the Samaritan woman's thinking (and ours) toward himself as the ultimate sanctuary, the spiritual site as well as the object of worship. It centers on Him and in Him. In fact, John's revelation (21:22) foresees the Holy City without a sanctuary "because the Lord God Almighty and the Lamb are its temple."

PRINCIPLES OVER PREFERENCES

In the light of that truth (better, Truth), the entire spectrum of worship is legitimized. The principles of worship become more important than our preferences in worship, and style takes a backseat to substance. To the degree that a given approach to worship anywhere along the spectrum violates the scriptural principles of worship—to that degree it loses value for all of us, no matter how drawn to that style we are. To the degree that a given approach to worship conforms to the scriptural principles of worship—to that degree it gains value for all of us, no matter how uncomfortable with that style we may be.

The principles of worship aren't difficult to discover. The Bible is not only a book *of* worship but also a book *on* worship.

All Worship Is God-Centered. The derivation of our word *worship* is the Old English word for *worth-ship*. We certainly aren't the worthy ones; He is (Rev. 4:11; 5:9, 12). Søren Kierkegaard's memorable metaphor endures because it captures this principle perfectly: Worship isn't a play in which the minister and the musicians are the actors, performing for our approval. If it is a play, our leaders are the prompters, we as a congregation are the actors, and God is the audience.[4] But if it's true that worship is all about Him and not all about us, why do we focus so much on worship style? That's the area least about Him and most about us—our preferences, our inclinations, our likes and dislikes!

Worship Is an Offering. This follows logically: If worship is all about Him, then it really doesn't matter how much I get out of it. What matters is how much I put into it. Perhaps the collection plate is a parable for the entire service: Beyond my money, what will I give to Him who is worthy "to receive . . . honor and glory and praise" (Rev. 5:12)? The divine bottom line is, of course, that we can't out-give God. The more we give, the more He gives, and we go home filled—*if* our focus all along was on giving instead of getting. If we "forget about ourselves and concentrate on Him and worship Him," as the worship chorus urges us, He won't forget about us.

Worship Is Work. Again, a logical progression: if I'm the giver, there's work to be done. I'm to be active. Once when I visited a nearby church, the worship leader began by saying, "Just sit back and enjoy the service." My reaction was immediate. I thought *"No!"* so quickly and so fervently that I almost wondered if I had unintentionally said it aloud. The pew is no place for a spectator, only for a participant. Otherwise, as the popular phrase has it, we're guilty of "idle worship." *Liturgy* means "the work of the people," and every church, even among the so-called non-liturgical churches, has a liturgy. It has work for the people to do in every service.

Worship Is Grounded in Scripture. Not only is Christ truth, but God's written Word is truth too (John 17:17). There we find revealed the One whom we worship, and there we find how best to worship Him. Paul wrote to Timothy, "Until I come, devote yourself to the public reading of Scripture, to preaching and to teaching" (1 Tim. 4:13). The evangelical church scores high on preaching and teaching, but how much Scripture is read in public worship? Would a visitor guess how high our regard for Scripture is?

Worship Is Both Adoration and Celebration. "Praise the Lord!" is the message of Psalms 146–150, as well as scores of other scriptural exhortations. In fact, the Psalter alone contains more than two hundred calls to praise. But the Bible balances praise with reverence, celebration with adoration. The last paragraph of Acts 2, the passage that has been one of the anchors of this chapter, reports the actions and attitudes of the Church immediately following Pentecost. As the New American Standard Bible translates, it's clear this was no transient emotion, "Everyone kept feeling a sense of awe" (Acts 2:43). In the exuberance of our praise, we dare not lose the awe. Liberian Christians have a wonderful call to prayer, "Let us drop beneath His feet." There is more to worship than lifting (or clapping) holy hands; there is also dropping beneath His feet.

This brief list is far from exhaustive, but the point is this: principles are more important than preferences in worship. Because they are, it's critically important for every worship style to examine itself honestly. If contemporary worship finds itself lacking in moments of reflection and contemplation; if liturgical worship is short on praise; if classical Protestant Christianity would be enriched by a personal testimony or two; if revivalism has neglected the sacramental commands of Christ, or forgotten the power of Christian symbols, or been oblivious to the spiritual benefits of celebrating Pentecost Sunday, or longed for more of God's Word to be read than just the preacher's text—it's time for a mid-course correction. There is room for movement along the line.

It will be impossible to sustain a war with our brothers and sisters in Christ if we will begin to appreciate and even appropriate the best of their traditions to enrich our own worship. Blended worship, seasoned with grace, can unify congregations while preserving transgenerational worship experiences. Just as the early Church blended seminal Christian liturgy (adapted from their roots in synagogue worship) with the overflow of the Spirit's moving among them, modern congregations can benefit by blending with the creative diversity around them.

A BENEFIT-COST ANALYSIS

To paraphrase G. K. Chesterton's comment on biblical Christianity, blended worship has not been tried and found wanting. It has been found difficult and left untried. Blending requires more planning, more patience, and more diplomacy than the typical church is accustomed to investing in its worship program. All of those are pluses, by the way.

It also requires the give-and-take of accommodation. When on the one hand, a senior saint hesitantly comes to accept a projection system and screen in the sanctuary, while on the other, her grandson finally concludes that affirming our faith in the words of the Apostles' Creed is not necessarily cold formalism, God is honored. As a matter of fact, the spirit behind those two examples sounds a lot like the numerous "mutuality commands" of the New Testament (see Romans 12:10 and 1 Peter 3:8, among many other passages that address our responsibilities to "one another").

I must add as well that blending requires more worship education, a ministry which all too often remains a "missing jewel" in evangelicalism. No one should be left out of the informational loop, wondering what's up with this Advent business ("Isn't that Catholic?") or pondering the meaning of that banner on the wall ("Do we use the fish symbol because Jesus called fishermen?").

Blending isn't easy, but the payoff is worth it. For some congregations, careful blending may eliminate the need for a separate service. Other churches may choose to retain alternative services but strengthen each service by borrowing the best from other worship traditions to create more balanced and inclusive, less idiosyncratic worship styles. For all churches, blending should mean an enhanced worship experience.

A SYNTHESIS OF FORM AND FREEDOM

One of John Wesley's greatest strengths was his genius for synthesis—finding the common ground between revivalism and social reform, between divine sovereignty and human freedom, between the established church and the religious societies, even between faith and works. Wesley was an instinctive centrist.

Why not a *worship* synthesis in that same spirit?

Why not a Wesleyan theology of worship which draws from the strengths of every point on the worship spectrum?

Why not a church of the center?

ACTION SUGGESTIONS

1. Create a worship committee for your church, with a mandate to do more than schedule special music or plan the annual Homecoming service. Work with this committee to analyze where you are and determine where you need to be in terms of the church's ministry of worship. This is the first step toward getting there.

2. Use more people in more ways during each worship service— reading Scripture, giving a prepared testimony, returning the offering plates to the front as a family, performing a drama, etc. Meet with these participants before the service—early in the week, if necessary—to review assignments and carefully coordinate details; this will also help them to understand the importance you are placing upon their contributions to the worship life of God's people.

3. Create a new worship tradition for your congregation, such as singing the Doxology each Sunday or affirming your faith in the words of the Apostles' Creed once a month.

4. Lead the congregation on a worship tour of their sanctuary, discussing the Christian symbols there, as well as liturgical centers like the baptistery and baptismal font, the communion table, the prayer rail, and the pulpit (or substitute). This could be done over several Sundays, in conjunction with a sermon series that demonstrates the origins of some of them in Scripture, or in the history and traditions of the Church.

5. Increase the frequency of the sacrament of communion and offer it in a variety of ways. For example, intinction (dipping the bread into the cup) lends itself to new designs for a communion service, as does taking the sacrament seated around a table.

FOR FURTHER READING

Dawn, Marva J. *Reaching Out without Dumbing Down: A Theology of Worship for the Turn-of-the-Century Culture.* Grand Rapids, Mich.: William B. Eerdmans Publishing Company, 1995.

Dawn, Marva J. *A Royal "Waste" of Time: The Splendor of Worshiping God and Being Church for the World.* Grand Rapids, Mich.: William B. Eerdmans Publishing Company, 1999.

Although Marva Dawn writes primarily for liturgical churches caught up in the worship wars, both her descriptions and her prescriptions are helpful for churches anywhere on the "worship continuum."

Ortlund, Anne. *Up with Worship: How to Quit Playing Church.* Nashville: Broadman & Holman Publishers, 2001.

This perennially popular "call to worship" has been revised and updated at least twice since its initial publication. Anne Ortlund makes worship, and worship renewal, contagious.

Webber, Robert E. *Blended Worship: Achieving Substance and Relevance in Worship.* Peabody, Mass.: Hendrickson Publishers, 1994.

Robert Webber, one of today's most prominent and prolific writers on worship, is sold on the blended service. This short study is an invitation to give it a try. A companion volume is *Planning Blended Worship*, published by Abingdon Press in 1998.

Willimon, William H. *Worship as Pastoral Care.* Nashville: Abingdon Press, 1979.

Here is a wonderful reminder of all the ways worship impacts the people in the pew—sometimes healing, sometimes prodding, sometimes inspiring, always (we pray) edifying—as the minister leads and lifts them to God in worship.

Zschech, Darlene. *Extravagant Worship.* Minneapolis: Bethany House, 2002.

One of the best composers of contemporary worship music has something helpful to say to everyone who worships, including those who are disenchanted with the Church.

NOTES

1. George Barna, *Revolution* (Wheaton, Ill.: Tyndale House Publishers, 2005), passim.

2. A. W. Tozer, *Worship: The Missing Jewel in the Evangelical Church* (Harrisburg, Pa.: Christian Publications, n.d.), passim.

3. Karen Aaker, "Beyond Contemporary Worship," *The McIntosh Church Growth Network Newsletter* 12, no. 1 (January 2000), 1.

4. Søren Kierkegaard, *Purity of Heart Is to Will One Thing* (New York: Harper and Row, 1956), 180–181.

8

The Church Jesus Builds Is
CATHOLIC

Amanda Drury

May they be brought to complete unity to let the world know that you sent me and have loved them even as you have loved me.

—John 17:23

[A]lthough a difference in opinions or modes of worship may prevent an entire external union; yet need it prevent our union in affection? Though we cannot think alike, may we not love alike? May we not be of one heart, though we are not of one opinion?

—John Wesley, *The Works of John Wesley*, Vol. V

E ach church my father and I passed in my hometown of Holland, Michigan, prompted a similar kind of question.

"Dad, are Lutherans going to heaven?"

"If they confess Jesus Christ as their Lord and Savior," was my father's reply.

"How about Baptists? Are Baptists going to heaven?"

Again he said, "Yes, if they confess Jesus Christ as their Lord and Savior."

"And Catholics?" I persisted. "Are Catholics going to heaven?"

With the same patience, my father repeated his mantra, "Yes, Amanda, if they confess Jesus Christ as their Lord and Savior."

I continued with these questions as we passed church after church—Presbyterian, Nazarene, Assemblies of God, Episcopalian, etc. And each time, my father gave me the same response. After I had exhausted my denominational options, he turned the question on me.

"Amanda, are Wesleyans going to heaven?" I knew the answer.

"Yes," I said, "if they confess Jesus Christ as their Lord and Savior."

My early attempt to divide the churches in my town into sheep and goats fell to the wayside of the deeper connections between the churches. Although I was young, my father was trying to instill in me that there was something much bigger and far greater than The Wesleyan Church I attended. I did not know it at the time, but I was getting my first glimpse of the Church catholic.

As Protestants, we often shy away from the term *catholic* (after all, we are not called Protest-ants for nothing). Those of us who use this term are often quick to give the disclaimer that we use it in a "small 'c'" kind of way. But as Alister McGrath points out, the Roman Catholic Church has no more claim on the word *catholic* than the Eastern Orthodox do on the word *orthodox*.[1] The term *catholic Church* is first recorded as used by Ignatius of Antioch (martyred in A.D. 110), who said, "Where Jesus Christ is, there is the catholic Church."[2] The word *catholic* simply means *universal* and refers to the Church of all times and places. This chapter will focus on joining this Church in preaching the whole gospel to the whole world.

WHY CATHOLICITY MATTERS

So what? What does it matter if we are working toward catholicity? After all, it is not even a biblical term. Local pastors have enough to worry about within their congregations; working on catholicity within the church is daunting enough. It can be overwhelming for pastors to think about catholicity in their communities, much less on a global scale.

While the word *catholic* may not be directly used in Scripture, the concept of unity is very much present. This unity is found in Jesus' extended prayer prior to his arrest:

> My prayer is not for [the disciples] alone. I pray also for those who will believe in me through their message, that all of them may be one, Father, just as you are in me and I am in you. May they also be in us so that the world may believe that you have sent me. I have given them the glory that you gave me, that they may be one as we are one: I in them and you in me. May they be brought to complete unity to let the world know that you sent me and have loved them even as you have loved me (John 17:20–23).

Jesus did not pray that his future disciples would exhibit strong leadership skills. He did not pray for discernment or personal piety. Jesus prayed that we would be *one*. Why? So the world may know of God's love. Catholicity is our greatest witness to a lost world.

If we are called to be one as Jesus and the Father are one, this raises the question of *how* the Son and the Father are one. Through our limited understanding of the Trinity, we see a relationship that is united but distinct. The Triune community consists of distinct persons with distinct missions in distinct relationships, yet all three are fully equal and united under the Godhead. Here we see that unity does not mean uniformity.

This understanding of unity with distinction is crucial in understanding the catholic Church today. The catholic Church that Christ builds does not throw differences aside, claiming, "Deep down we are all saying the same thing." We are not. There are differences. There are real differences between Wesleyans and Presbyterians, between Arminian and Reformed doctrines, between Protestants and the Roman Catholic Church. Being the catholic Church does not mean we glaze over our differences; rather, we recognize these differences and acknowledge that something even greater unites us.

John Wesley's classic sermon "Catholic Spirit" demonstrates this unity with distinction within the Church. Wesley openly admitted that finding unity is difficult in that we do not think alike nor do we act alike, but then went on to explain, "Although a difference in opinions or modes of worship may prevent an entire external union; yet need it prevent our union in affection? Though we cannot think alike, may we not love alike? May we not be of one heart, though we are not of one opinion?"[3]

Wesley then acknowledged various differences in the Church while maintaining his desire and obligation for unity:

> I believe the Episcopal form of Church government to be scriptural and apostolical. If you think the Presbyterian or Independent is better, think so still, and act accordingly. I believe infants ought to be baptized and that this may be done either by dipping or sprinkling. If you are otherwise persuaded, be so still, and follow your own persuasion. It appears to me, that forms of prayer are of excellent use, particularly in the great congregation. If you judge extemporaneous prayer to be of more use, act suitable to your own judgment . . . I have no desire to dispute with you one moment upon any of the preceding heads. Let all these smaller points stand aside.[4]

Wesley not only was willing to put aside variations in practice; he went so far as to make known his determination not to ask "whether you allow baptism and the Lord's supper at all," and then to declare, "Let all these things stand by."[5] Wesley did not allow even the avoidance of the sacraments to keep us from finding this catholic spirit.

What matters, he wrote, are the questions, "Is thy heart right with God? . . . Dost thou believe in the Lord Jesus Christ? . . . Dost thou know Jesus Christ and him crucified?"[6] Wesley readily acknowledged differences in opinion and practice, but maintained that these differences must not keep us from finding unity in Christ.

THE WHOLE GOSPEL

Christians are better equipped to share the whole gospel because of our differences. When asked what distinguishes The Wesleyan Church from other denominations, one of our primary answers most likely would be the emphasis we place on holiness. The Wesleyan Church has been entrusted with this gift of pursuing holiness. That is not to say other denominations do *not* pursue holiness; however, few churches outside the historic holiness denominations pursue holiness in such an intentional and reflective way. Social holiness, personal piety, and perfect love are some of the many attributes The Wesleyan Church and her sister denominations strive toward. The Wesleyan/Holiness movement has been entrusted with this wonderful gift; it is our responsibility to share it with the Church catholic. We are a much needed piece in this gospel puzzle. The catholic Church needs us to share this gift, just as we are in need of the gifts that are well pursued in other denominations.

Part of preaching the whole gospel is listening to our brothers and sisters, using their gifts to supplement our weaknesses in order that we may present the gospel fully and clearly. Without the interaction of the gifts of other denominations, we run the risk not only of becoming schismatic (separated from the Church catholic), but also of becoming heretical.

To be a heretic is not precisely the same as being unorthodox. Heretics are *within* the Christian tradition. Atheists, agnostics, or those belonging to other religions would not fall under the category of "heretic." The problem with heretics is not the absence of Christian truth in their lives, but that they take *part* of the truth and mistake it for the whole.

If The Wesleyan Church were to become schismatic, separating itself from the catholic Church, we may fall into the heresy of making holiness the whole, rather than part of the gospel. Then, not only would The Wesleyan Church risk heresy by not being connected to the catholic Church, but we would risk enabling the catholic Church to become heretical because we were not sharing our gift of holiness.

Some fear that extensive interaction with other denominations may weaken our Wesleyan identity. Fear of the mainline churches overpowering our holiness heritage may stand in the way of pursuing catholicity. I heard such fears from well-intentioned people when I began seminary at a mainline institution. Interestingly, I found that through my interactions there, my holiness roots were deepened. I did not lose my identity; I sharpened my identity as I was able to see the distinctions, and dialogue about my holiness understanding and this mainline way of thinking.

By interacting with the Church catholic, we gain a greater understanding of who we are and where we are going. We are reminded of the crux of our faith: the work of Christ that unites us all, as well as the distinctive points of our faith that serve as rich gifts by which we can bless the larger Church.

What does it look like to share this Wesleyan gift? This means we are actively seeking to be a part of the catholic Church in local, national, and worldwide settings. Being a part of the catholic Church means we are actively pursuing relationships with other churches in our local settings. While Wesleyan ministers enjoy fellowship with other Wesleyans at various Wesleyan functions, such as conferences or continuing education courses, we should pursue similar relationships through involvement in local ministeriums and other forums.

We experience a false unity if we are content to limit our fellowship only to other Wesleyans.

Jesus' prayer makes the startling claim that the best way to share God's love with a lost world is not through evangelistic strategies or better programming, but through the unity we share with our fellow brothers and sisters in Christ. If our ministers are not leading the charge in this area, we cannot expect more from our congregants.

Of course, being the catholic Church goes beyond being neighborly with the church down the street. We can pursue catholicity on national and global levels as well. Perhaps we could consider joining the National or World Council of Churches. Perhaps this means we would take a greater role in future projects like The Wesleyan/Holiness Study Project. As a denomination, we can be actively seeking both official and unofficial avenues toward catholicity.

To be the catholic Church means we are conversing with churches on local, national, and global levels. It means we are actively seeking opportunities to share the gifts we have been entrusted with, while benefiting from the gifts of others. To be the catholic Church means we find unity with distinctions so that we might proclaim the whole gospel to a lost world.

THE WHOLE GOSPEL TO THE WHOLE WORLD

Naturally, the gospel cannot be preached to its fullest if it is being preached within a limited scope. Part of being the catholic Church means preaching the whole gospel to the whole world. Preaching the whole gospel to the whole world means we are actively sharing the gospel with women and men of every race from every economic status (Gal. 3:28).

CLASS

I remember the fight that broke out amongst my fellow kickball players in fifth grade. It was in the middle of recess, and a teacher rushed over to our field to investigate the ruckus. I do not remember what lofty rule of kickball had been breached, prompting the argument, but I do remember the complaint of one member of the opposing team: "It's all the rich kids against us poor kids." As I glanced around at my teammates, I realized she was right. Out of all the kids in my fifth grade class, I was on the wealthier team. At the time, I found it odd that all of the wealthier kids *just happened* to end up on the same side.

Our teams were picked in the traditional style: Team A picked a player, Team B picked a player, and so on, with each team alternating their picks until both teams were complete. It was not just the wealthier students that had chosen to play together, but the poorer students as well. Even at this early age, we were showing our desire to homogenize.

In the early 1950s, Donald McGavran revolutionized churches worldwide through his findings on what he called "the homogeneous unit principle." The basic premise of this principle was that churches needed to be built around homogeneous units of people. Dr. McGavran is known for his statement that people "like to become Christians without crossing racial, linguistic or class barriers."[7]

This prompted the work and writings of C. Peter Wagner, who followed up McGavran's thesis with the books *Our Kind of People* and *Your Church Can Grow*. Wagner argued that people needed to feel "at home" in their faith and that imposing culture upon those who are different was a form of imperialism. Wagner went so far as to state that "segregation is a desired end."[8] Perhaps most convincing in McGavran's and Wagner's proposals was the evidence that churches operating under this homogeneous unit principal showed greater growth. Pragmatism seemed to have the final say. The greater the homogeneity, the higher the attendance.

But growth is not necessarily a sign of obedience. A growing church of congregants who look and live alike is not necessarily a sign of an obedient church. In an article in *Christian Century*, Ralph H. Elliot confronted this principle by a reference to Jürgen Moltmann's *Religion, Revolution and the Future*. Elliot summarized Moltmann as saying,

> [If the church is to be authentic, it] must be heterogeneous, reconciling the educated and the uneducated, black and white, high and low. Moltmann sees the church at its best when it contradicts the natural groupings of human beings, while Wagner sees the church as at its best when it conforms to such groupings.[9]

The catholic Church consists of men and women of various races and economic backgrounds. There are no social divisions, and there are no caste systems. While each local church cannot represent the entire catholic Church, we are capable of approximating the vision by including all within her walls. In order to preach the whole gospel to the whole world, we must preach to both women and men, to those of all races, and to those from various classes.

RACE

North Americans have the unfortunate history of appeasing our consciences by sending missionaries to Africa while participating in "white flight" at home, moving our congregations from the city to the suburbs. We are not the catholic Church because we have a Wesleyan sister church in Sierra Leone. We are the catholic Church because we *worship* with those of all races, even in our local communities.

The catholic Church that Jesus builds knows no difference between Jew and Gentile, black and white, Asian and Russian. While the catholic Church *knows* no differences, the catholic Church *looks* different. Here again we see that unity does not equal uniformity.

Are we pursing racially reconciled worship in our communities, or are we content merely to support foreign missions? The second greatest command is to love our neighbors as ourselves. While we can spiritualize this command by claiming to love the neighbor we have never met, we dare not at the same time ignore the neighbor who is literally right next to us. We cannot love *in abstracto*.

I imagine most pastors would value a diverse congregation. In fact, I imagine many pastors would love to diversify their congregations. In most cases, desire is not the issue; it is transforming that desire into a reality that proves to be difficult. If we want to diversify our churches to emulate the catholic Church, we must trade in our good intentions for intentionality. We must become advocates instead of supporters.

We can start by asking ourselves concrete questions: When was the last time I had a meal with someone of another race? When was the last time my church partnered with a local church of another race? Do I share my pulpit with guest preachers of another race? Am I praying for racial reconciliation in my community?

Pursuing racial reconciliation within the church means we pursue worship with equality. Being a part of the catholic Church means we worship with one another, we listen to one another, and we inquire about one another.

Members of a well-intentioned white, middle-class church recently visited a dilapidated section of their city to perform acts of service for the many black families who reside there. Partway through their reconstruction of a run-down porch, the owner approached the workers. She was a single mother, and she was not happy. "Did I ask you to fix my porch?" she demanded.

"No," came the hesitant reply.

"Well, then why are you fixing my porch?"

"It was broken," the church people responded.

"You know what I need more than a fixed porch?" the woman demanded.

Again, an uncomfortable, "No."

"Food for my kids," she said, her voice softening. "Why didn't you just ask?"

Although well-intentioned, the members of this church saw themselves as community saviors who could swoop into the lives of the people in this neighborhood, perform their good deeds, and then return to their church with their consciences appeased.

The catholic Church knows no difference of race. It is racially inclusive—a characteristic of the Church, for which most of us should be eternally grateful. The parable of the workers in Matthew 20:1–16 tells the story of how the early morning workers in the vineyard received the same pay as those who came to work the vineyards late in the day (much to the chagrin of the initial workers). Those of us who are Gentiles are the latecomers. We were invited into the catholic Church through the gracious invitation of the Jewish Messiah, Jesus Christ. Remembering this hospitable invitation extended toward us encourages us to cross racial lines in our worship, service, and proclamation of the gospel.

GENDER

The catholic Church consists of men and women preaching the whole gospel. Being the catholic Church means we preach the gospel to men and women and allow both men and women to preach the gospel. One of the forefathers of The Wesleyan Church, the Reverend Luther Lee, participated in ordaining Antoinette Brown, a Congregationalist, as the first female minister in America in 1853, preaching the ordination sermon for her, which was entitled "The Woman's Right to Preach." This is yet another reason why the Wesleyan voice is needed in the catholic Church, to testify to the Holy Spirit's outpouring on women.

When women are welcomed into the church, they need to know they are full contributors to the gospel, not second-rate citizens. If we are going to discourage women from preaching, we must also discourage women from baptism, the symbol of our unity and new life in Christ.

Being a part of the catholic Church means allowing for the Holy Spirit to breathe into the lives of both men and women to preach the gospel. This Church, which was birthed at Pentecost, emerged by the pouring out of the Spirit on all flesh. The catholic Church consists of men and women upon whom the Holy Spirit has fallen.

JESUS' FINAL WORD

This idea of preaching the whole gospel to the whole world is daunting. Catholicity sounds unattainable—yet we are left with Jesus' last prayer that we might exhibit this catholicity in order that the world may know God's love. May it be as You have said, Lord.

ACTION SUGGESTIONS

1. Spend time praying for unity in God's church on local, national, worldwide levels. Pray that God will open your eyes to breaches in unity and give you wisdom to know how to respond.

2. Foster friendships with those who are different from you in both race and class. This can be as simple as sharing a meal together.

3. For pastors: Get involved in a local ministerium. If one does not exist in your area, contact neighboring pastors to meet monthly for coffee and prayer.

4. For pastors: Share your pulpit with someone of another race or gender. Allow your congregants to hear the Word of God from another vessel.

5. For pastors: Plan together and lead your church in partnering with another local church to perform a needed service in your community.

FOR FURTHER READING

Barth, Karl. *Dogmatics in Outline.* New York: Harper & Row, 1959.
This book comprises Barth's lectures, which follow the outline of the Apostles' Creed. While a number of books are available on this topic, this is one of my favorites. *Dogmatics in Outline* is a great introduction to Barth's theology.

Bonhoeffer, Dietrich. *The Communion of Saints: A Dogmatic Inquiry into the Sociology of the Church.* New York: Harper & Row, 1963.
If you are familiar with Bonhoeffer's *Cost of Discipleship* or *Life Together*, you may enjoy this earlier work. This book was one of Bonhoeffer's dissertations and establishes theoretical foundations for his later, practical works.

Drury, Keith. *There Is No I in Church: Moving Beyond Individual Spirituality to Experience God's Power in the Church.* Indianapolis: Wesleyan Publishing House, 2006.
Drury openly addresses and critiques the current trend to bypass the catholic Church in favor of a private, individual relationship with God. This accessible book is a great resource to address this issue in group settings.

Kung, Hans. *The Church.* New York: Sheed & Ward, 1967.
No study of the Church is complete without this classic text. Kung is a modern Catholic who provides his readers not only with a look at all four classic attributes of the Church, but also an extremely insightful look at the priesthood of all believers.

Wesley, John. "Catholic Spirit," *The Works of John Wesley,* vol. V. Grand Rapids, Mich.: Baker Book House, 1978.
In this short sermon, Wesley calls for his listeners to move beyond differences in sacramental practices and to find unity in Christ.

NOTES

1. Alister McGrath, *Christian Theology* (Malden, Mass.: Blackwell Publishers, 2001), 500.

2. Ibid.

3. John Wesley, *The Works of John Wesley,* vol. V (Grand Rapids, Mich.: Baker Book House, 1978), 493.

4. Ibid., 499.

5. Ibid., 497.

6. Ibid.

7. Donald A. McGavran, *Understanding Church Growth* (Grand Rapids, Mich.: William B. Eerdmans Publishing Company, 1970), 198.

8. C. Peter Wagner, *Leading Your Church to Growth*, as quoted in Ralph H. Elliot, "Dangers of the Church Growth Movement," *Christian Century* 25 (August 12–19, 1981), 800.

9. Elliot, "Dangers," 799.

The Church Jesus Builds Is

SPIRIT-LED

❀

Ken Schenck

*There is one body and one Spirit—just as you were called to
one hope when you were called—one Lord, one faith,
one baptism; one God and Father of all.*

—Ephesians 4:4–6

*A particular Church may, therefore, consist of any number of members,
whether two or three, or two or three millions. But still, whether they be
larger or smaller . . . [t]hey are one body, and have one Spirit, one Lord,
one hope, one faith, one baptism, one God and Father of all.*

—John Wesley, "Of the Church," Sermon LXXIV

The book of Acts is better than a history of the early Church. It is the early Church as seen through the eyes of the Holy Spirit. A dispassionate history of the early Church easily might get bogged down in conflicts at which the book of Acts barely hints of taking place. A penetrating comparison of Acts with Paul's writings gives us strong indications that the early Church was messier than we might think from the book of Acts alone. While some dream of getting back to the way things were in the early Church, it is perhaps just as likely that the early Church was as full of carnality and conflict as any church today.

At the same time, our desire to "get back" to the church of Acts is legitimate because what Acts actually does is show us what the church *should* be like. Acts 15:36–41 may not tell us what we learn from Galatians 2:13, that Paul and Barnabas disagreed over more than whether they should take Barnabas' cousin John Mark on the second missionary journey. But what Acts *does* tell us is how Christians can agree to disagree and go on to accomplish tenfold what they would have accomplished otherwise. Rather than wade into the gory details of a historical conflict, the Holy Spirit, as reported by Luke in Acts, accentuates how Christians should settle their differences.

The book of Acts begins as the continuation of the Gospel of Luke, "In my former book, Theophilus, I wrote about all that Jesus began to do and to teach" (Acts 1:1). The wording is tantalizing. Is Acts then about the things Jesus *continued* to do and teach? How so? The answer appears in 1:8, "You will receive power when the Holy Spirit comes on you; and you will be my witnesses." Accordingly, we are not surprised to read Luke reporting in 16:7 that "the Spirit of Jesus" directed the mission of Paul and his companions.

Of course, it would take the Church several hundred more years to work out the details of how the Holy Spirit and Jesus were related within the one God, but the book of Acts already clearly represents the continued work of Jesus through the Holy Spirit in the Church. It is no surprise that some have suggested that the name "Acts of the Apostles" is a misrepresentation. What we really have here are the "Acts of the Holy Spirit."

Therefore, we must see the Holy Spirit as the main character in the story of Acts. It is the Holy Spirit who defines the Church, empowers the Church, and directs the Church. And the Church Jesus continues to build today is defined, empowered, and directed by the Holy Spirit, as it always has been—if it truly is to be regarded as the Church.

THE HOLY SPIRIT DEFINES THE CHURCH

When Peter told the crowd on the Day of Pentecost what they should do in the light of recent events, he suggested two things, "*Repent* and *be baptized*, every one of you, in the name of Jesus Christ for the forgiveness of your sins." In response, promised Peter, God would perform the key action, "And you will receive the gift of the Holy Spirit" (Acts 2:38, emphasis added). In Acts, as well as in Hebrews and in Paul's writings, the most significant element in becoming a part of the new people of God, the *sine qua non* of Christian identity, is the Holy Spirit. Paul, in Romans 8:9, indicates that "if anyone does not have the Spirit of Christ, he does not belong to Christ." Similarly, 2 Corinthians 5:5 recognizes the Spirit as "a deposit, guaranteeing what is to come." In the language of the King James Version, the Spirit here is an "earnest" that secures our inheritance, while further allowing us to taste of the stuff of heaven (Heb. 6:4). He is God's "seal of ownership on us" (2 Cor. 1:22).

Throughout the book of Acts, the key factor in persons joining the people of God is the reception of the Holy Spirit, also phrased as being "filled" with the Holy Spirit and being "baptized" in the Holy Spirit. Just before the beginning of Jesus' ministry, John the Baptist had said, "I baptize you with water. But one more powerful than I will come . . . He will baptize you with the Holy Spirit and with fire" (Luke 3:16). This promise was fulfilled on the Day of Pentecost, as Acts 1:5 intimates. None of the disciples had received the Holy Spirit before that day and thus could not be Christians in the "technical" sense. The Day of Pentecost is rightly called the birthday of the Church.

In the rest of Acts, we will find that new believers did not fully enter the company of the people of God until they received the Holy Spirit. This fact is most poignantly seen in Samaria, where a number of individuals had been baptized but had not yet received the Holy Spirit (Acts 8:16). One of them was Simon the sorcerer, of whom

Peter said, "Your heart is not right before God . . . I see that you are full of bitterness and captive to sin" (8:21, 23). Acts leads us to believe that Peter and John went to Samaria primarily because these baptized individuals had not yet received the Holy Spirit (8:14–16), a problem of inclusion into the people of God that needed to be addressed. These individuals had moved toward God, but they were not yet fully "saved."

In Acts 10, Gentiles received the Holy Spirit even before they were baptized, to the amazement of the circumcised believers with Peter (10:45). Long before the debates over whether Gentiles need become Jews to be saved, God settled the issue of inclusion by putting His seal of ownership on them. Peter immediately recognized the implication: they were members of the people of God. "Can anyone keep these people from being baptized with water? They have received the Holy Spirit just as we have" (10:47). Years of study committees, General Conferences, and "ratification by the districts" were preempted in one swoop by the Holy Spirit. Gentiles were in, even without being circumcised.

It would be easy for Western individualists to forget that these instances of receiving the Spirit were not simply individual experiences. Paul asked the Corinthians, "Don't you know that you yourselves are God's temple and that God's Spirit lives in you? . . . God's temple is sacred, and you are that temple" (1 Cor. 3:16–17). The "you" in these instances is not singular, but plural. It would actually miss the heart of Paul's point if we took these expressions to be about you or me as individuals. Paul was talking about the way Christians relate to one another in the "body" of Christ, which he would later identify as the Church, in his letter to the Colossians (Col. 1:18, 24; Eph. 4:4). The Church collectively is the body of Christ; the Spirit in and of that body is the Spirit of Christ. It is not that individual bodies do not also house the Spirit, but this individual indwelling is secondary and derivative of the Spirit dwelling in the Church as a whole.

Therefore, the Spirit defines the Church. If one wants to know how to define the Church catholic, the Church universal, the Church invisible (that is, in the sense that it is not defined by denominations or church buildings), the answer is this: the Church consists of all those who, since the Day of Pentecost, have partaken of the Holy Spirit and have either held their confession of faith firm until the end (Heb. 3:14), or now daily continue to run with patience the race set before them. The Church is the temple of the Spirit on earth and in heaven, the communion of all the saints of all the ages.

THE HOLY SPIRIT EMPOWERS THE CHURCH

The Wesleyan tradition has long understood correctly that the coming of the Holy Spirit involves purification. As Acts 15:9 says of the conversion of the Gentiles, God "made no distinction between us and them, for he purified their hearts by faith," giving them the Holy Spirit. But the book of Acts interestingly puts its emphasis on the *power* that the Holy Spirit bestowed upon the disciples in order that they could be effective witnesses to Christ's resurrection. Jesus said, "You will receive power when the Holy Spirit comes on you; and you will be my witnesses in Jerusalem, and in all Judea and Samaria, and to the ends of the earth" (Acts 1:8). Of course, the apostles had a unique witness to bring to their generation: "With great power the apostles continued to testify to the resurrection of the Lord Jesus" (4:33). In other words, they were able to use their personal and collective experience of Him following His resurrection. But we notice throughout Acts that others who accepted their first-person testimony also bore this same witness under the power of the Holy Spirit; a prominent example is Stephen (6:10). The power to witness that comes from the Holy Spirit was not limited to the first apostles.

So we see that one of the primary manifestations of the power of the Holy Spirit in the Church comes in the form of witness. "Unschooled, ordinary men" like Peter and John (4:13), individuals who were hiding just a few days previously, now stood boldly before the Jewish ruling council proclaiming, "Salvation is found in no one else, for there is no other name under heaven given to men by which we must be saved" (4:12). The Greek-speaking Stephen could pray for the forgiveness of his murderers as he was being stoned, because he was full of the Holy Spirit (7:60). And Paul could speak boldly, not only before the Sanhedrin in Jerusalem, but also before governors and even before the Roman emperor, because he, too, was full of the Holy Spirit (23:11).

In our day, God still expects His Church to speak out, not only in witness to Christ and salvation, but surely also to work for change in society and in the world. James wrote, "Anyone, then, who knows the good he ought to do and doesn't do it, sins" (James 4:17). Of all the New Testament authors, James would include within "the good" effecting real change in the world, just as Jesus himself did for the downtrodden of Galilee, while He was on earth. Luke 4:18 gives us a kind of "inaugural address" for Jesus' ministry; here, quoting Isaiah 61:1, Jesus announced He had come "to preach good news to the poor . . . freedom for the prisoners and recovery of sight for the blind." The witness of the Church for Christ is not simply a matter of enacting laws to restrict the behavior of others, but, more importantly, it is proclaiming and evidencing the power of the Spirit to change the hearts and minds of others for the better.

The witness of the apostles in Acts did not come simply by way of bold words. More striking is the way the Holy Spirit empowered the church to do miraculous deeds, which both transformed the lives of individuals and demonstrated God's endorsement of their broader message about Christ. It is no coincidence that immediately after the

Day of Pentecost we find Peter and John healing a lame man (Acts 3). Clearly, this man's life was changed forever. He is a reminder that in the middle of eternal purposes, God wants to touch the needs of solitary individuals through the church. Yet this miracle also gave witness to Christ in such a way that about two thousand more Jews became believers because of it (4:4).

Throughout the rest of the book of Acts, the Holy Spirit performed miracles of this sort through the believers. Just as Jesus (Luke 5:17–26; 13:10–13) and Peter (Acts 3:1–10; 9:32–35) had healed lame men and women, so Paul healed a lame man (Acts 14:8–10). Just as Jesus had raised several from the dead (e.g., Luke 8:51–56), so in Acts both Peter (Acts 9:36–43) and Paul (20:7–12) raised persons from the dead. These dots through the New Testament form a line extending beyond New Testament times to what the Holy Spirit can do through the church today as well. The books of Luke and Acts especially emphasize that even the things Jesus did on earth, He did through the power of the Holy Spirit (e.g., Luke 4:18; Acts 2:22). We believe, of course, that Jesus in His divinity could have done these things in His own divine power. But apparently, He chose to "play by the human rules" in His miracle working—indeed, even in His resurrection.[1] The point is that Jesus, Peter, and Paul did nothing through the power of the Holy Spirit that, in theory, the Church today could not do as well.

THE HOLY SPIRIT DIRECTS THE CHURCH

The power that the Holy Spirit gives is not a mindless power. When Peter, Stephen, or Paul stood up, full of the Holy Spirit, to speak before the Sanhedrin, the Spirit did not just give them a mindless power to use according to their own wisdom and thinking. Rather, we should understand that the Spirit was empowering and directing their wisdom and words, as well. Luke 12:11–12 says,

"When you are brought before synagogues, rulers and authorities, do not worry about how you will defend yourselves or what you will say, for the Holy Spirit will teach you at that time what you should say." The gospel of John states the same idea in this way: "The Counselor, the Holy Spirit, whom the Father will send in my name, will teach you all things and will remind you of everything I have said to you" (John 14:26).

The Holy Spirit thus directs the thoughts and the thinking of the Church. We have seen this already in the coming of the Holy Spirit upon the uncircumcised Gentiles in Cornelius's house (Acts 10:44). We would love to have such clear statements of direction today when churches deliberate on important concerns that arise in the flow of history. In this case, God not so subtly showed the Church that not only Jews, but Gentiles also, can be Christians. So when the issue was formally brought up in the Jerusalem Council, the matter actually had been decided already by divine vote (Acts 15:6–11).

We scarcely can continue to believe what we believe if we do not affirm that the Holy Spirit has continued to direct the thoughts of the Church—not only in the days of the New Testament, but also in the years that have followed. Indeed, we cannot consider the New Testament itself to be authoritative over our lives if we do not accept that the Holy Spirit worked through the Church to affirm *these individual books* as constituting an authoritative collection. If the Church would not have been trusted to handle this crucial task, then each of us individually would have to decide which books are the authoritative Word of God, from among all books, ancient and modern.

In another example of the Holy Spirit's continuing direction of the Church, the text of the New Testament itself was not even able to arbitrate between Athanasius and Arius when they debated the Trinity. Both could point to various individual biblical texts in support of their diametrically opposed arguments. Only if we have faith that the Holy Spirit helped the Church through those crucial controversies can we have full confidence in the things nearly all Christians everywhere believe.

The Holy Spirit, as profiled in the book of Acts, not only directs the thoughts of the Church, but directs its actions as well. When Paul was trying to determine where he was to go next on his missionary journey, the Holy Spirit forbade him to go into Asia (Acts 16:6). The Holy Spirit told Philip to go up to the chariot of the Ethiopian eunuch (8:29), then whisked him away to Azotus afterward (8:39–40). We have no reason to believe the Holy Spirit does not continue to lead, not just individuals, but also denominations and, indeed, the Church universal, in these same ways today. Nothing at the end of Acts suggests that God has stopped leading us individually or corporately through the Spirit, nor does it suggest that the Spirit of Jesus does not still work in this way.

John Wesley rightly saw that God's directive activity in our lives begins long before we ourselves become aware of it. He used the phrase "preventing grace," or prevenient grace, for the grace of God that is at work in our lives even before our individual conversions, which leads us, whether individually or corporately, to be in the right place at the right time. Mordecai's question to Esther long has echoed this understanding, "Who knows but that you have come to royal position for such a time as this?" (Esther 4:14). Paul himself believed God had "set [him] apart from birth and called [him] by his grace" (Gal. 1:15). In other words, sometimes God is at work to bring us to a particular place so we can effect His will when the *kairos* moment comes.

But how much more is His grace at work in the Church! We find ourselves easily applying Wesley's understanding of prevenient grace to our own individual lives, but how much more important and likely it is that God leads His Church in this way, even without our knowing so! This is not to say that every direction a local church—or even the

Church catholic—takes is God's best will. But surely it means that the overall movement of the Church universal, over time, is God-directed, and that the individual movements of smaller groups within that broader Church also are most frequently directed by God.

The Church today could use a look in the mirror to recognize that, in fact, it is only the Church to the extent that it is filled with the Holy Spirit. If any part of the visible Church would look in the mirror and not see the Holy Spirit within it, then it must come to the shocking realization that it is not, in fact, a part of the true Church. If any part of the Church were to look in that mirror and fail to see any power of the Spirit reflected, whether of boldness in speaking out or in action, then it must acknowledge a major identity crisis. If a part of the Church does not rely on the Holy Spirit for its direction, then that part of the Church is headed in the wrong direction. However, since we are not the ones who ensure the movements and actions of the Holy Spirit, we need never fear that the true Church universal will not advance. The most important task for us as individuals and denominations is to make sure that we are a part of that which God will do with us or without us. The Spirit in God's Church is on the move today, as He was in the days recorded in the book of Acts. Let us move with Him.

ACTION SUGGESTIONS

1. Take some time to reflect on the witness of the Spirit in your own life. John Wesley did not believe all individuals necessarily sensed the Spirit's witness that you are a child of God immediately when you became a Christian. But he believed you would soon come to a point where you realized that you are in fact a child of God. Take a moment this week to reflect on the work and presence of God in your life.

2. Now where do you see the witness of the Spirit *in your church*? Since we are collectively as well as individually the temple of God, we should be able to discern the fruit of the Spirit and the witness of the Spirit corporately as well as individually. Where do you see the witness of Christian identity in your church? Suggest that your congregation set aside some time to reflect on the corporate witness of the Spirit among you and to discern where the fruit and gifts of the Spirit are in your midst.

3. What are some ways in which either you or your church have underestimated the power of the Holy Spirit? Is there an area that you have individually or corporately failed to believe that God can do it? Is there a sin or temptation that you have not trusted God for victory? Set aside some time this week to "ponder anew what the Almighty can do."

4. Are there any areas in your life or in the life of your church where you have not trusted in the Lord for direction? Take a moment to rehearse five decisions you have made either individually or collectively in the last 10 years. Did you turn to the Spirit at any point in that process? Determine that you will factor more prayer into any decisions you are in the process of making right now and that you will trust that the Lord is guiding us even when we do not fully sense Him.

FOR FURTHER READING

Dunn, J. D. G. *Baptism in the Holy Spirit*. Philadelphia: Westminster, 1970.

Moltmann, Jürgen. *The Church in the Power of the Spirit: A Contribution to Messianic Ecclesiology*. Philadelphia: Fortress, 1993.

Oden, Thomas. *Life in the Spirit: Systematic Theology.* Vol. 3. San Francisco: HarperCollins, 1992.

Pinnock, Clark. *Flame of Love: A Theology of the Holy Spirit.* Downer's Grove, Ill.: InterVarsity, 1996.

NOTES

1. It is important to note the way that Luke in Acts, Paul in Romans, and the author of Hebrews, phrased and conceptualized their declarations of Jesus' resurrection: "God raised Him from the dead" (e.g., Acts 2:32; 3:15; 4:10; 10:40; 13:33; 17:31; Romans 4:24; Hebrews 5:7).

A RESPONSE

TENSIONS THAT STRENGTHEN THE CHURCH

Wayne Schmidt

Now to him who is able to do immeasurably more than all we ask or imagine, according to his power that is at work within us, to him be glory in the church and in Christ Jesus throughout all generations, for ever and ever! Amen.

—Ephesians 3:20–21 (TNIV)

Sir, you wish to serve God and go to heaven? Remember that you can not serve him alone. You must therefore find companions or make them; the Bible knows nothing of solitary religion.

—John Wesley

For years now our local church has had the privilege of being a simulcast site for the annual Willow Creek Association Leadership Summit. This past year featured a captivating and somewhat controversial interview with Bono, lead singer of the band U2, who is known worldwide as both a rock star and a philanthropist.

Bono was interviewed by Bill Hybels, chairman of the board of the Willow Creek Association. Hybels expressed gratitude for the way Bono had enlarged his heart for the world and spurred his involvement in the AIDS crisis in Africa. In turn, Bono admitted that

Hybels had challenged him to consider the role of the Church in addressing the needs of the world. Hybels passionately believes the local church is the hope of the world. Bono stated that while he has loved and admired Christ, he has not felt that way about the Church.

When Bono declared he had previously loved the Christ, but couldn't stand the Church or Christians, the audience gathered on our site snickered. Their reaction bothered me more than Bono's statement! Was it a nervous laugh? Did these leaders of over one hundred different local churches think it was funny? Is it a sign that even leaders of the Church have surrendered to the cultural conclusions that the Church is at best a dysfunctional family, hopelessly idiosyncratic and beyond redemption?

This distinction between feelings about Christ and the Church is not new. As I grew up in the 1960s, the Jesus People proclaimed their love for Jesus, but not for His Church. This sentiment is easily received in our highly individualistic, postmodern culture. It allows people to marinate in their cynicism while developing a self-absorbed walk with God.

I am unashamedly a lover and admirer of the local church. This love is not blind; it's discerning. The Church is both led and filled with fallible human beings. But it is also the Bride of Christ, and I find it biblically untenable that one can love the Groom (Christ) and despise His Bride (the Church).

I'm grateful that Wesleyan scholars have undertaken this endeavor to clarify and communicate a Wesleyan ecclesiology. These scholars obviously love the Church of Christ, yet speak prophetically to those of us who bear responsibilities for leadership. I also believe the "low view" of the Church in our world today presents us with a great opportunity. The opportunity can be captured in the following formula:

Experience > Expectations = Value

When people's experiences exceed their expectations, they perceive it as adding value to their lives. With expectations so low for the Church today, we have the opportunity to introduce and involve people in church experiences that exceed those expectations and add value to their lives.

But why is a Wesleyan ecclesiology important for pastors? As Amanda Drury's chapter powerfully points out, we are not claiming to have a corner on how the Church is to exist and expand. But we do have a unique contribution; she refers to it as the "Wesleyan gift" to the larger Church. We who lead churches in the Wesleyan movement are stewards of this gift to the Church at large and to the world yet to be redeemed.

For me, as a local church pastor, two "gifts" contribute to my deep connection with Wesleyan ecclesiology, which I'd like to surface in this chapter.

OPTIMISTIC GRACE

We steward the gift of "optimistic grace" to the broader Church. As Amanda Drury points out, Wesleyan churches pursue holiness in an intentional and reflective way (p. 141). This optimistic grace boldly proclaims that people can experience both conversion *and* transformation. Believers not only attain a new position in Christ, but actually become new persons in Christ as well. We experience not only the grace that brings forgiveness of sin, but also the grace that empowers us to resist the temptation to sin. This optimistic grace, which allows us to love God truly with all that we are and to love our neighbors as ourselves (Mark 12:29–31), creates a holy expectation that we can be changed in this life, not just in the life to come.

This optimistic grace transcends mere individual experience, as important as that is. It extends to the Church's capacity to incarnate Christ. Pastors and lay leaders who see their communities through the lens of this grace envision their churches as bright lights in even the most darkened and hopeless of surroundings. We boldly believe people are best served, not when the church is marginalized in their lives, but when it is prioritized.

However, optimistic grace does not justify a state of denial about the human flaws present in the church. It should not create a church culture of "terminal niceness," which involves glossing over pressing problems with pious platitudes. Such "happy talk" sentences churches to a life of limited effectiveness and fruitfulness. But the trumpet call we sound is much more of a reveille than "Taps."

This optimistic grace should lead us not only to holy expectation, but also to fuller consecration. Wesleyan churches expect God to show up when they worship, and they stand ready to surrender to the loving demands of their King. We anticipate answers to our prayers and simultaneously practice prayer as a means of searching our hearts and inviting God to occupy every crevice of our spirits. When faced with the most hopeless of personal or community situations, we expect the Holy Spirit to usher in a hope that is fortified, as we commit to being fully available to Him.

In several ways, the academic contributors have provided us practitioners with a framework to build prevailing churches that are places of optimistic grace. We need these frameworks, lest we bow at the altar of pragmatism. Churches experience whiplash when they seek only to maximize the latest tools and trends, while ignoring the truths and themes that have made the Church "the Church" throughout all generations.

So I call upon us to expect more from God in our local churches. This is not the power of positive thinking, but of transformed living. We are to incarnate the Lord of the Church, who spoke with such authority and lived with such love that it altered the course of history. I'll never forget two simple words boldly displayed in a church I visited early in my ministry, almost twenty-five years ago: "God can." The fact that

"God can" invites me to be "strong and courageous" as I serve His church. Even when our strength to serve fails, God reminds us as He did the Apostle Paul, "My grace is sufficient for you, for my power is made perfect in weakness" (2 Cor. 12:9).

THE TENSIONS THAT STRENGTHEN THE CHURCH

The Wesleyans have given another "gift" to the Church and world. This gift finds its genesis in our founder, John Wesley. Bob Black highlights this gift in his chapter on worship, stating, "One of John Wesley's great strengths was his genius for synthesis . . . [He] was an instinctive centrist" (p. 133). Wesley could live with tension; Black cites the examples of divine sovereignty and human freedom, as well as revivalism and social reform. Living with such tension may have made his systematic theology more complex, but it created energy in his ecclesiology that resulted in transformation of individual lives in the most desperate of situations, which spread the movement to the world.

As I read the contributions of the scholars, I began to note several tensions that call us as practitioners to join Wesley in creating synthesis. No doubt, this will add some complexity to our ministry. Many of us serve in contexts that tend to be "either/or" and are not very receptive to "both/and." Throughout history, the Church has been known for its pendulum swings, which have led it to extreme positions that eventually required corrective action. While the latest pendulum swing may sell books and fill how-to seminars, it also can rob the Church of its redemptive momentum.

TENSIONS THAT STRENGTHEN
ATTRACTION → ← MISSION

Recent Church history reflects a pendulum swing from attraction to mission. When I had the privilege of helping to found our church in 1979, mega-churches were just beginning to emerge. Their services were planned to connect with and impress those who were seekers. Church facilities were designed to feel familiar to those who had grown up without a church experience. Programming emphasized relevance to the "felt needs" of the spiritually uninformed or unresolved. One of the first conferences I attended as a rookie pastor was hosted on the campus of the Crystal Cathedral by Robert Schuller, perhaps the ultimate spokesperson at that time for ministry through attraction. The emphasis on attraction seemed to reach its zenith in the 1980s and 1990s.

Today there is a reaction to this attraction model of ministry. Many reference it in condescending tones as they call for an approach that is missional. Programming is a dirty word. Church facilities are to be avoided, or they are perceived as a necessary evil that should be spartan at best. The focus on felt needs is being supplanted by a preoccupation with humanity's fallenness and brokenness. Ministry does not happen within the walls of the church; it happens beyond the walls of the church.

During our twenty-fifth anniversary year as a local church, 2004, we recognized we had not adequately emphasized the mission side of this tension. Actually, this was more than our recognition; we sensed it as a fresh revelation from the Spirit of God. Like most churches, we'd begun in rented facilities. After four years of very challenging work, our church had grown to about 150 attendees. Then we undertook the challenge of building our first facility. In our community at that time, facility equaled credibility. While it took us four years to grow to 150 in attendance, it took us only one week after opening our new facility to double that number. Over the next twenty years, we experienced relocation and seven different building programs, funded by multiple capital campaigns. We grew from being perceived as a community church to a regional church with broader influence in the larger city.

But in a time of reflection and prayer on the day that marked twenty-five years of my pastoral ministry at the church, God impressed upon me that while many celebrated our church's accomplishments, our community was more unchurched than it had been when we started. We were actually losing ground in our mission of community transformation, while having the appearance of success.

So we started asking a bold question: What would it take to *permeate* our community with the good news of Jesus Christ in a way that develops disciples? We began to focus on what would be necessary for every person in our region to have a relationship with an authentic believer and to have an opportunity to make an informed decision about whether to place his or her faith in Christ. We began to identify missional strategies we believed God was revealing to us, and then brought them together in a package and format that we now call "VP 2020," our Vision Path 2020. Our purpose is to permeate our entire community with the good news of Christ by the year 2020. Having sensed a lifetime call to this local church, and having thought of that "lifetime" in terms of the oft-used biblical number of forty years, the year 2020 would be a transitional time in my life—and I delight in our efforts to permeate our community by then.

So the strategies began to unfold. "The Earlier the Better" strategy focused us on children and youth—those ages that tend to be most receptive to the gospel—who then can make other life decisions in light of their faith decisions. But we were no longer measuring only the church attendance of children and youth; we also began to ask how we could make an impact at every elementary, middle, and high school in our region.

The "Love Your Neighbor" strategy moved us beyond simply challenging our members to invite people to church, to challenging them to become hospitality hosts in their neighborhoods, building relationships through which witness could be shared.

"New Churches Reach New People" led us to commit to planting a new congregation every year. Because we recognized that we could never permeate the community with one style and from one address, we planned to plant the churches in a variety of settings with a variety of styles.

"Community Partnerships for Compassion Ministries" served as a catalyst to join with other faith-based and secular organizations to touch the lives of those most needy and at risk in our region.

"Media for Ministry" provided the recognition that not all people will be reached through strategies that are primarily relational, and technology could help us connect with those who would seek to take initial faith steps in privacy.

The pendulum was swinging. We talked less about *seating* capacity and more about *sending* capacity. Yet we felt checked—to fulfill our mission would require a strong "base camp." On our campus, people of all ages would be exposed to the vision, worship, and equipping opportunities that would empower them to be salt and light in their neighborhoods, on their campuses, and at their workplaces. We need to continue to attract people in order to provide certain dimensions of their development as disciples, so we can then send people as "missionaries" into their spheres of influence.

This attraction → ← mission tension is addressed in some form by all of the scholars. Mike Walters treats it extensively in his chapter on Incarnation, as does Mike Fullingim in his chapter on mission. I believe it is also a tension found in Scripture. In the Old Testament the predominant emphasis is on attraction, as God developed a people who would gain the world's attention and draw others to Him as the one true God. In the New Testament the predominant emphasis is on mission, as God's people were empowered to be His witnesses to the ends of the earth (Acts 1:8) and were dispersed by persecution. As leaders, we find the synthesis between these tensions as they feed each other, rather than standing in opposition to each other. We "draw in" seekers and believers to build them up as disciples so they can be "sent out" to impact their worlds for Christ.

ALREADY → ← NOT YET

In his chapter on eschatology, Joseph Coleson highlights the hope embodied in the "already and not yet" nature of God's people and kingdom. We recognize that the fulfillment of many biblical promises is already a historical reality and yet anticipate the day when all promises will be "realized fully, gloriously, and eternally" when Jesus fulfills His promise to return bodily to this earth and inaugurate His eternal reign of righteousness and peace.

It seems to me that some denominational expressions of the catholic Church place more emphasis on the "already" nature of the Kingdom, and others on the "not yet" nature. I also believe that most expressions of the Wesleyan movement tend toward the "not yet" nature of the Kingdom, and that we must move more toward the "already." The optimistic grace fueling the Wesleyan movement calls us to expect God to work in greater ways in the here and now.

Jim Garlow, senior pastor of Skyline Wesleyan Church, has observed that while the Wesleyan/Holiness and Pentecostal movements share the same roots, the Wesleyan/Holiness branch has tended to emphasize the *purity* the Spirit brings, while Pentecostals highlight the *power* the Spirit releases. In terms of the tension now under consideration, I think Wesleyans have tended to embrace the "not yet," while Pentecostals lean toward the "already." Does this enlarge the faith of Pentecostals that God will act in the present tense?

As a pastor, I find that this is not merely a philosophical consideration. Right now, I'm challenged with this tension. Over the past twenty-five years, our immediate community surrounding the church has gone from less than five percent people of color to being almost twenty-five percent ethnic minorities. Yet, sadly, our church family has not changed to reflect our community, and our desire to permeate our city is facing racial barriers.

Do I as a pastor, and does our congregation corporately (a dimension of Keith Drury's chapter highlights), have the faith to believe that we can overcome racial barriers here and now? We know the Great Commission calls upon us to "make disciples of all nations [*panta ta ethnei*, all the ethnic groups]" (Matt. 28:19), and we are sent out in the authority of Jesus. Yet repeatedly I've been told, as we've begun our intentional efforts to be more diverse, that it is impossible for an existing congregation to make this transition. While we may worship together in heaven one day "from every nation [Gr. *ethnos*, or ethnicity], tribe, people and language" (Rev. 7:9), on earth we'll remain segregated. The "homogeneous principle" (p. 144) tells us our congregation will be weaker and grow more slowly (or even decline) if we try to diversify.

But in this case, and in other dimensions of church life, I think the pendulum has swung too far to the "not yet." I'm calling upon our congregation (and myself) to act upon the belief that God can do a miracle in our congregation on earth, not just in heaven. It will be a slow process, but we're believing and risking that the small seeds of this Kingdom endeavor will blossom.

OTHER TENSIONS THAT STRENGTHEN

Many other possible tensions to explore are highlighted in the earlier chapters of this book. Here are a few more I'm continuing to synthesize myself:

Mystery → ← *Measurement*. What can a church actually measure, and what might it never be able to measure, as it seeks to track its faithfulness and fruitfulness?

Being → ← *Doing*. While Mike Walters effectively argues for an emphasis on *being* (p. 33), isn't it often through *doing* things in obedience that we incarnate Christ individually and corporately?

Consonant → ← *Dissonant*. In what ways does the church need to emphasize themes consonant with the culture, as a source of connection with people (relevance), and in what ways do we need to speak prophetically to create a dissonance that differentiates Christian life from cultural values (revelation)?

Individual → ← *Corporate*. While Keith Drury appropriately highlights the need for a corporate emphasis, how do we as church leaders serve as spiritual directors in helping individuals determine next steps of development in ways that not only strengthen them personally, but also strengthen the church as a whole?

After reading this book on Wesleyan ecclesiology, and penning this chapter, I'm thinking about printing a new title on my business card: "Optimistic Synthesizer." While it will puzzle everyone else, it will remind me of the blessing of belonging to a branch of God's Church that embraces His optimistic grace and wrestles with the creative tensions that ultimately strengthen the Church.

ACTION SUGGESTIONS

1. Do you agree that our culture today, both inside and outside the Church, tends to devalue the Church as a "dysfunctional family, hopelessly idiosyncratic and beyond redemption"? List several specific ways we can be honest with ourselves about the Church's shortcomings, yet affirm its biblical position within God's redemptive plan.

2. A formula for creating value has been expressed as

Experience > Expectations = Value

List some of the low expectations people have for the church, relating to its various purposes: worship, fellowship, discipleship, serving, evangelism, etc. How might your church exceed those low expectations, creating value for those seeking Christ through your local church?

3. This chapter contrasts the attractional model of ministry with the missional model of ministry. List several differences you see between the two. List some dangers of emphasizing one without the other. Suggest potential abuses or pitfalls within each approach. Consider how your church could implement both approaches effectively.

4. Do you know the percentage of unchurched people in your community? If not, decide to find out. Is this percentage growing larger or is it shrinking? What strategies could your local church develop to permeate your community with the good news of Jesus Christ?

5. This chapter lists several tensions that actually strengthen the Church when synthesized. Which of these tensions stands out as being most valuable for your local church to enhance intentionally? Does one of these tensions currently threaten the health of your church because of imbalance to one side or the other?

FOR FURTHER READING

Chilcote, Paul Wesley. *Recapturing the Wesleys' Vision*. Downers Grove, Ill.: InterVarsity Press, 2004.

As the introduction states, "Wesleyan theology has an important contribution to make to contemporary Christianity as a whole. It is a 'both/and' rather than an 'either/or' theology, a bridge-building tradition that can speak with clarity and healing to an age of serious division in God's family" (p. 11).

Hull, Bill. *The Disciple-Making Church*. Old Tappan, N.J.: F. H. Revell Company, 1990.

This book provides a comprehensive strategy that values both the attractional and missional dimensions of discipleship, applying the incarnational ministry of Christ to the disciple-making efforts of a local church.

Rusaw, Rick, and **Swanson**, Eric. *The Externally Focused Church*. Loveland, Colo.: Group Publishing, 2004.

We've discussed this book as a staff and board, as we seek to be more missional as a church. It's a very practical and thorough resource for any church with the God-honoring intention to permeate its community with the gospel.

Snyder, Howard A. *The Radical Wesley and Patterns for Church Renewal*. Downers Grove, Ill.: InterVarsity Press, 1980.

This book provides a wonderful orientation to Wesley's ecclesiology and capacity to hold theological concepts in tension. Snyder includes a section with very practical applications for the Church today, which is still very relevant though the book was written over twenty-five years ago.

11

BUILDING BRIDGES

Donavon W. Shoemaker

Just as each of us has one body with many members, and these members do not all have the same function, so in Christ we who are many form one body, and each member belongs to all the others.

—Romans 12:4–5

Send down thy heavenly grace into my soul that I may be enabled to worship thee, and serve thee as I ought.

—John Wesley, 1825:11, *Prayers for Children*

In 1966, Peter Scholtes published his song "They'll Know We Are Christians by Our Love." It's not sung much these days, but its declaration of the incarnational Church is still relevant. As Mike Walters writes in his chapter about the Church being the visible imitation of Jesus, so the unity and love for one another that Jesus both commanded (John 13:34) and prayed for (John 17:21) is an advertisement that the body of Christ is united in Christ.

THE FOUNDATION IS CHRIST

This love for one another does not originate from the believer, but rather from Christ himself, through the Holy Spirit living within the believer. This love that God purposed for the body of Christ to manifest gives powerful witness to Jesus Christ. His answer to

Philip's request, "Lord, show us the Father" (John 14:8), was that everything anyone needed to know about the Father could be discerned by knowing Jesus himself (John 14:9–11).

In like manner, Jesus' plan is that people will recognize Him through their interfacing with His Church. He stated, "No branch can bear fruit by itself; it must remain in the vine. Neither can you bear fruit unless you remain in me. . . . This is to my Father's glory, that you bear much fruit, showing yourselves to be my disciples" (John 15:4, 8). In other words, we show ourselves to be His disciples because we are His disciples. Our doing comes from our being. Any attempt to produce fruit by striving to be "religious" will ultimately be revealed for the play-acting it is.

A proverb often repeated, concerning a child and a parent says, "The apple doesn't fall far from the tree." This is similar to the phrases "Like father, like son" and "a chip off the old block." Often, one can observe a child's appearance, personality, and responses and recognize or identify the parent. I have experienced occasions when I knew who a preacher's mentor was by observing mannerisms, choices of words, and preaching style. In similar manner, the fruit the Church produces will reveal the One in whom we "have our being" (Acts 17:28).

A LOCAL CHURCH CAN BUILD BADLY

Unfortunately, a local congregation can become something less than the Church Jesus desires to build. Then the fruit it bears may be carnal rather than incarnate, and Jesus cannot be identified through it. When this happens, those outside the church begin to question the Kingdom's authenticity and to voice the mistaken generalization that the church differs little from any other community institution. Even many within the church become hurt, confused, and disillusioned.

A congregation in my community went through more than a year of conflict in which a group of members picketed outside the church.

Every Sunday, and on other days when there were services, a group of disgruntled members stood outside with placards and a bullhorn, declaring that the pastor was an unfit leader. As it happened, the newly installed pastor had replaced the offering tellers with people of his choosing. (Reportedly, the offering totals increased immediately.) The ensuing leadership battle within the church became so serious that they had to hire a private security service to guard the doors and ensure the safety of worshipers. The conflict became a court matter and church elections were conducted by a retired judge with no ties to either side. During this discord, the pastor allegedly received many threats upon his life; even guest preachers received calls warning them not to come to the church. I preached there during the fracas, and though I had to walk by the picketers, I was not harmed. Peace finally emerged out of this long conflict, but, of course, it did nothing to enhance the community's understanding of how Christians are to love one another!

As Mike Walters stated, true followers of Jesus are recognized "by the depth of their love for one another" (p. 36). However, we are prone to drift from our "first love" and become subject to operating in the realm of worldly practices and principles, as Jesus charged the church in Ephesus with doing (Rev. 2:4). Churches sometimes focus more on money than salvation, membership than discipleship, position than servanthood, vocation than calling, competition than oneness, and accolades than glorifying God. Such failure jeopardizes the church's incarnational testimony and hinders our effectiveness in bringing the lost to a place of experiencing salvation—our central assignment, as Mike Fullingim discusses in his chapter on the missional church.

The question arises whether such failure creates irreparable damage to a church's incarnational testimony. While it does hinder, God knows how to restore His church, and thus its testimony, back to health. For God to do this work, the church must humble herself, and in contriteness, acknowledge wrongdoing, ask forgiveness, and, when necessary, make restitution (Isa. 66:2). Keith Drury, in his chapter on being one holy Church, speaks of God using various means of grace "to make us become what we aren't yet" (p. 72), which includes correction and sanctification. When the church is humble and repentant and seeks God, the world will once again begin to recognize that which is real, that which embodies Jesus himself.

BUILDING WELL, INTENTIONALLY

I have found it necessary, periodically, to step back and reflect on what we as a local church, and I as a pastor, are being and doing in relation to what God wants. I've found myself driven to ask, "What comes to mind when people think about our church? What do people see when they see me? Do they see Jesus? Are we intentionally building bridges that can span any resistance—across which, by our being, doing, and testimony, we can introduce people to Jesus Christ?"

I came to First Wesleyan Church in Jersey City in 1972, arriving in the midst of the neighborhood transitioning, which was largely related to racial matters. Long-term residents were relocating to the suburbs or to other smaller cities and towns. First Wesleyan had diminished in numbers, impacted by an exodus of its members.

Many churches in the neighborhood were so decimated that they ceased to function and sold their buildings to congregations who either had been renting or were in need of larger facilities. First Wesleyan was in a stronger position than many; the congregation had several African-American families already in leadership positions. Additionally, my predecessor was an international graduate student at Drew University, who was gifted cross-culturally and possessed a remarkable ability to befriend people and build bridges of trust in a relatively short time. He viewed the demographic change in the community as an opportunity, whereas many viewed it with despair. He was not afraid to go into the streets, to knock on doors, or to visit local parks to introduce himself, the congregation, and most importantly, Jesus Christ to those he encountered.

Over the years I've met several people who, upon learning where I pastor, have begun to reminisce about having attended either a kids' program at the church or a fresh air program sponsored by the church, in which children spent two weeks in the country with families from churches in central New York. They have also commented about the pastor "back then," who was from Australia. As I have listened to these recollections and observed body language as these people have talked, I know their memories are delightfully positive. Through these encounters, they saw the body of Christ at its best and caught a glimpse of Jesus himself.

I came to Jersey City as a novice, fresh out of seminary. I was young, idealistic, and probably immature, with limited exposure to urban and cross-cultural ministry. The experience I had came from working at a YMCA while attending college, and participating with my wife, Vi, in a three-month internship in Chicago, while in seminary, through a program called "Urban Ministry Program for Seminarians" (UMPS). Additionally, I had received very helpful classroom training relating to urban, cross-cultural ministry while in seminary, including a several-day field trip to Chicago. These experiences confirmed in my spirit what God was calling me to do and helped prepare me. I came to Jersey City with a desire to be a bridge-builder—building bridges of trust across mistrust, and building bridges of love and acceptance over divisions of hate, hurt, and rejection. I also saw this as the church's mission in a neighborhood of transition.

BUILDING WELL REQUIRES COMMITMENTS

Though I arrived in Jersey City with limited understanding of what I was about to face, I did bring with me insights from a seminary professor, from the pastor I served under in Chicago, and from others I met in the UMPS program. I have found their insights to be wise and helpful, both in rebuilding an existing church and in building bridges in a changing neighborhood.

A COMMITMENT TO RESPECT A CHURCH'S TRADITIONS, HISTORY, AND LEADERSHIP

When transition begins in a neighborhood, the church most likely will find itself lagging behind in making the changes needed to reach her new neighbors. Change is not easy to implement. Many churches in transition are in such a precarious condition that sweeping changes can create circumstances in which nearly everyone abandons ship. Other congregations may choose not to change at all, which leads to isolation from the community.

The pastor needs to know—or the new pastor needs to learn quickly—who in the congregation has influence and ask for their support in presenting his or her vision of what the church should be in the community. If the leaders of the church agree on this vision, it is easier to gain support from the other members in implementing needed changes.

Being young and inexperienced, and coming into a church with a lot of history and tradition, I had to be patient in introducing changes that would make our services more appealing to those we were already reaching and to those we hoped to reach. As I was interviewing for the position, one member of the board challenged me with the question, "Are you going to come in here and try to change everything like some of the other ministers?" I committed myself that I would respect the leadership and existing practices, although some change would be necessary and inevitable.

The value of changing slowly instead of rapidly is that it gives everyone time to pray, unify, reflect, and envision what is really needed, which minimizes resistance. When we at Jersey City First Wesleyan look back, we see that considerable change has taken place, and continues to take place as our neighborhood continues to transform. However, this has been done without the "shedding of blood" that so often occurs. The key member of influence at our church was once asked how he felt about the changes that had taken place at First Wesleyan. He responded by saying that while he did not like all of the changes, he chose not to stop them because he believed they were necessary for the church to grow and to reach more people for Christ.

A COMMITMENT TO PRESENCE AND IDENTIFICATION

If a church is to be effectively incarnational in an urban, multicultural neighborhood, the majority of its members, leaders, and pastors need to live in it, or at least live very close to it. More and more clergy in our community are living out of town, commuting ten to fifty miles to their churches. An increasing number of members of our local churches are moving outward as well, purchasing homes or renting apartments because they are more affordable, or because they see it as an improvement to their quality of life. An increasing number of members drive in to services and help support the church financially, but their ability to minister outside the church walls, in our community, is greatly diminished.

Living in the neighborhood increases interaction, commonality, and recognition. When we live in the area we are seeking to impact for Christ, we cross paths with people at the grocery, at the bank, at city hall, and at department and convenience stores. Also, when we live in a community, we desire to invest more in that community, especially as we see God's purposes in our being there. Over time, as people see our credibility, we gain their confidence and trust.

First Wesleyan has been known for years as a community church; in times of crisis and grief, neighbors have turned to us, even if they aren't members. Some would object to this practice and turn non-members away, but such openness truly helps to build bridges. We have made our facility available, without charge, to block associations, tenant groups, HIV/AIDS support groups, ministerial groups, and other community organizations.

A COMMITMENT TO STAYING

A church situated in a changing community will build bridges when it communicates that it is committed to staying in that community. When I came as pastor to Jersey City, I was asked over and over when the church was going to close and sell. We had groups offering to purchase the building. Multiple times, I personally was asked how long I was going to stay. When we experienced a burglary, people said, "I guess you'll be getting out of here soon." Some feared my vacations would become times to look for another church. But nobody says or thinks these things anymore regarding the church or me. They know we are committed to being here.

I realize no one is married to a local church for life; I myself have been a part of five churches in my lifetime. But when it comes to ministering cross-culturally, making a long-term commitment of at least a few years is invaluable. It takes time to overcome prejudices and build credibility.

A COMMITMENT TO LISTENING AND LEARNING

We cannot build bridges by disregarding the foundations and fabric that make up a community. We need to know its demographics, along with its history, its politics, and its religions. While some of that information can be gained through census reports and reading histories, the best knowledge is gained by interacting with people, especially for someone who has come from another community, church, culture, or race. Building bridges across unfamiliarity is possible, if we are willing to listen and learn—but it does take time. We need to put agendas and prejudices aside and intentionally seek to be open-minded. As I have listened to others who are different from me, I have been able to understand better their worldviews, which are shaped by different histories and cultures than my own. We never can fully understand another culture, but we can understand enough to build bridges across the barriers that have for too long kept the Church divided.

A COMMITMENT TO COLLABORATION, NOT COMPETITION

First Wesleyan is a local church that not only has survived the dramatic demographic changes in our community, but has also produced fruit nourished from the heart of God. We have grown numerically, though we are not large. Presently, we face new challenges as the demographics continue to change.

I have attended pastoral gatherings at which, upon learning I serve in an urban church, people ask about our social programs. I get embarrassed, as our programs are similar to those of many churches outside the city. In fact, some churches elsewhere have more organized social programs. We do give food to hungry people; provide counseling, and support; and encourage and assist individuals with AIDS. Most of these things we do in the fashion of being a "good Samaritan," rendering help as needed, much as Donald Wood describes in his apt phrase, the "everyday work of believers who sound no trumpets" (pp. 118–119).

In fact, starting a social service in a church may not always be prudent; other programs in the community may already be fulfilling a given need very well. In such instances, our more effective role may be working in cooperation by referral, by encouraging our members to volunteer, and even by encouraging and providing financial support. Our volunteering, for example, will enable our members to meet and help the people we want to serve. Collaboration multiplies the resources available to meet needs; competition should never be our intent, anyway.

What we do is not about First Wesleyan, and what you do is not about your local church. It is about building bridges for the kingdom of God, which is done in a myriad of ways, a few of which we have discussed here. To quote Donald Wood again, the Church is on earth to "multiply the number of compassionate incarnations of the Word" (p. 119).

ACTION SUGGESTIONS

1. Ask yourself the following questions, taking the time necessary to reach complete and honest answers:

- When I think of the local church I belong to, what do I think about it?
- What do those who do not attend our church think about it?
- The body of Christ is to be incarnational; how is the incarnate Christ evident in our church?
- What is the character of the community around our local church? Does our church reflect the community in its cultural and ethnic makeup? If not, why?
- What do we have in common with our community? How are we different? How might our church intentionally and effectively build bridges across cultural and other long-standing barriers?

- If most of us live elsewhere, would I, or would any of our members, be willing to move into the community we are trying to reach?

2. When you have begun to deal seriously with these questions and the ministry mandate they represent, begin to present them to others in your church. Introduce them in your preaching; make time on the agenda of a church board meeting for discussion; and call a meeting of interested persons to begin a "vision-casting" process.

FOR FURTHER READING

Bakke, Ray. *The Urban Christian: Effective Ministry in Today's Urban World*. Downers Grove, Ill.: InterVarsity Press, 1987.

Based on Bakke's personal journey, this is a manual on living and doing ministry in the city.

Claerbaut, David. *Urban Ministry*. Grand Rapids, Mich.: Zondervan, 1983.

I cut my teeth in urban ministry on this practical book. Because it is out of print, you may find it difficult to find, but if you do, it will richly reward your search.

Lingenfelter, Sherwood G. and **Mayers**, Marvin K. *Ministering Cross-Culturally: An Incarnational Model for Personal Relationships*. Grand Rapids, Mich.: Baker Book House, 1986.

This book is highly regarded by many involved in cross-cultural ministry.

12

WE LOVE YOUR CHURCH, OH GOD

Colleen R. Derr

> *Just as each of us has one body with many members, and these*
> *members do not all have the same function, so in Christ we who are*
> *many form one body, and each member belongs to all the others.*
>
> —Romans 12:4–5

> *We love the place, O God,*
> *Wherein Thine honor dwells;*
> *The joy of Thine abode*
> *All earthly joy excels.*
>
> —William Bullock

We join with this old hymn in saying, "We love your Church, oh God." Our passion for her health and prosperity consumes us. We spend our hours and days contemplating improvements and adjustments that will make her more effective. We debate the avenues of change to make her stronger. We hold her under a microscope, inspecting the furnishings, the methods, and the programming to make her better. We spend hours in mental and verbal conversation about her, exert extreme energy for her, and give unselfishly of ourselves to her. We truly do "love the place."

THE CHURCH IS MORE THAN A SINGLE PROGRAM OR FOCUS

What is "the place" for us, though? When we think of this place, the church, what comes to our mind? Do we see bricks, parking lots, shrubbery and carpet color? Do we think of sewer systems (currently, my local church has a serious issue with this), furnishings, and decorations? Perhaps we see programs and ministries. Then to us, the church is Sunday school, worship service, nursery, choir, midweek prayer meetings, Bible studies, and vacation Bible school. For some, the church may be a focus, such as evangelism, missions, youth ministry, worship, or outreach service ministries. Others may see it in terms of a specific church culture, personality, style, and form.

We all see the church differently, based on our own preferences, perspectives, and passions—and we tend to define it by our focus on one element. When I think of church, I think of kid's spaces: colorful walls, interactive stations, little chairs, music with motions, puppet stages, and lots of activity. For me, the church is her children.

I have a passion for children, and the call on my heart is to see every child given the opportunity to experience God's love through a caring church. It is my consuming drive. I truly believe we can transform our world one child at a time, and the transformation takes place in a thriving local church. Supporting the church in every way and any way that can help to make that possible has become my life calling. This passion has led me to focus on children and the church's ministry to them to the extent that I can lose sight of the Church Jesus wants to build, as I hide it behind the church *I* want to see built.

Children's ministry is not all the church is or can be. When my oldest daughter, Jerica, turned thirteen and headed into the terrain of questioning belief and making faith personally hers, my perspective on church grew. Suddenly, she thought the songs we sang were stupid, and the games we played were lame; certainly, the chairs were too small. It didn't take me long to realize that the church needed to offer her more than children's ministry, which resulted in me gaining an appreciation for a solid youth ministry. Now as my husband and I engage my senior parents, my now-young-adult daughter, my teenage sons, and my youngest daughter, I realize church is far greater than what's right in front of my eyes, and my perspective has been enlarged again. The eight of us have different ideas on what church is and what it should be. None of us is necessarily wrong about what we see, but none of us is completely right either, because church isn't just what fuels our personal passions or fills our individual needs; the church is greater than that.

It is easy to become consumed with a specific area of service within the church, as I have done with children's ministry; we tend to focus on the minute, the momentary, what's right in front of our eyes. When we devote all our energy and time to enriching and improving one microcosm of church life, we can come to define and measure the entire church through that one element. Our own programs and pet ministries can become the priority. When our view of church becomes too narrowly focused on children, missions, worship, stewardship, evangelism, or outreach, we tend to forget the church is not just one of these, but all of them together. These many parts create a perfect whole. God places within each of us a passionate desire for service and ministry, yet He intends our ministry to be lived out in the church, not in isolation. Christ's intention for the church embraces all our passions and desires, and fulfills all our needs. His view of the church goes far beyond the immediate and the instant. We need to see the church as Jesus does; we need to see His big picture.

THE CHURCH JESUS BUILDS THROUGH US

The reminder hardly can come too often: what we need is clearer vision, broader vision, better vision, *Jesus'* vision. We need to grasp more fully His desire for the church, His church. We cannot lose sight of whose church it is, and His standards for her. This book offers a glimpse into just that, as it examines the scope of all the church truly is called to be, and the needed reminder of whose church it truly is. It is His to build through the Spirit working in us, and ours to build only through Him; the Church Jesus builds is incarnational and eschatological, holy, missional, nurturing, worshipping, compassionate, catholic, and Spirit-led.

The church is still God's greatest single instrument for reaching a lost world. Para-church organizations, with their single-focus approach to ministry are worthwhile and necessary, but they are not the church. There is a power in the all-encompassing scope of the church that goes beyond a para-church organization's ability. The church in its fullest extent offers Christ through hands of healing to a hurting world, arms of comfort to the sad, words of affirmation and acceptance to the lonely—reaching out beyond our physical and mental walls to all God's children, in love. The church incarnate is found in local elementary schools, helping kids who struggle with math and parents who struggle with English. The church incarnate is food shelters and senior centers, hugs to hurting children, and listening ears to struggling teens.

Jesus' church is also eschatological, a big word for a children's pastor, but also a reminder of where our hope lies. Let us embrace the transformation in our perspective from doing ministry in the moment to living ministry out in the "already and not yet," fully claiming the benefits and promises of God that are available to us today while looking forward to the hope of tomorrow. Let us operate under the umbrella of expectancy, excitement, and anticipation, knowing God is actively at work and believing in His immanent return. The church living in the "already and not yet" responds to the urgency of our quest by making sure our content is solid and biblical, and that we are not merely babysitting or entertaining.

A church that embraces corporate holiness and sanctifies itself anew will be a beacon of hope and peace, welcome to and in our neighborhoods that are in trouble. The church's relevance is based less on furniture choice and song selection than on our being a loving, caring, compassionate body of believers, fully embracing a community in need. Our relevance lies in caring enough to discover what needs to be done, as well as being committed enough to exert the energy and resources to see it accomplished. Relevance is a church making a difference in our own lives today, causing us to affect others where they live, and offering them compassion when needed.

The urgency of the message and the compassion that grows out of holiness propels Jesus' church to be missions-minded, looking outward to children, teens, and adults without the Savior. Mission evangelism permeates every program and outreach event so that in everything said and done, we present the gospel as a church burning with a passion to reach the lost.

The evangelism that occurs from a missional mindset is partnered in the church with Bible-based teaching that is foundational and relevant. The church's teachers understand that our moments are fleeting and that the message of the world is louder than it used to be. These teachers recognize the challenge of imparting practical biblical wisdom that matters, while creating strong relationships and providing opportunities for service. Their teaching moves us beyond ourselves and into genuine kinship with other believers.

I love children and my God-given focus is on them, but I love "the place" more and understand fully the need to embrace all Christ wants for her—not dividing or segmenting the church, but capturing the full scope of all she was intended to be. These pages offer the challenge to study, know, and feel the grandeur of the Church Jesus is building, to hear the call to broaden our perspectives, to enlarge our mindsets, and to move beyond the ordinary, to His extraordinary expectations for her, now and eternally. Teach us to love Your church, oh God.

ACTION SUGGESTIONS

1. Construct a mental image of your church. What does it look like? What elements do you see? Are these elements physical? Are they programs? Are they people? How does your mental image line up with the Church Jesus wants to build? Are you missing any elements?

2. Read 1 Corinthians 12:12–27 with your church in mind. Consider how the complete body of Christ is manifested in your church.

3. Open a dialogue with several attendees of your congregation from various age groups. Ask them to describe their image of church. Compare and contrast your images of church with one another's.

4. Answer the following questions: In what tangible ways is your church incarnational? Eschatological? Holy? Missional? Nurturing? Worshipful? Compassionate? Catholic? Spirit-led? What specific steps might your church take to be and do better?

FOR FURTHER READING

Hybels, Bill. *Courageous Leadership*. Grand Rapids, Mich.: Zondervan, 2002.

Schmidt, Wayne. *Ministry Momentum*. Indianapolis: Wesleyan Publishing House, 2004.

Schmidt, Wayne, and others. *The Pastor's Guide to Growing a Christlike Church*. Kansas City: Beacon Hill Press, 2004.

Stanger, Frank Bateman. *The Church Empowered*. Grand Rapids, Mich.: Francis Asbury Press, 1989.

These are only a few of the best resources I've found over the years; each has helped to produce and form my love of the Church.

ABOUT
THE AUTHORS

ROBERT BLACK is a third-generation Wesleyan minister. Since 1986 he has been a member of the religion faculty at Southern Wesleyan University; for ten years he served as chair of the division. A graduate of Southern Wesleyan University, he also earned the M.Div. degree from Asbury Theological Seminary and a Ph.D. in Church History from Union Theological Seminary in Virginia.

Bob has been a contributor to the Wesleyan Bible Commentary Series (1 & 2 Timothy), to *Reformers and Revivalists*, the denominational history of The Wesleyan Church, and to several reference works in his field. *How Firm a Foundation*, his history of Southern Wesleyan, was published for the university's centennial celebration in 2006.

Bob and his wife, Judy, are the parents of Jon, Jenny, and Jared and the grandparents of Olivia, the world's greatest grandchild.

JOSEPH COLESON was ordained in the Northwest District of The Wesleyan Church in 1979. His B.A. is from Indiana Wesleyan University, and his M.A. and Ph.D. degrees are from Brandeis University. He has been a professor of Old Testament at Nazarene Theological Seminary since 1995; previously, he was on the faculties of Roberts Wesleyan College, Rochester, New York, and Western Evangelical Seminary, Portland, Oregon. His pastoral experience is in four congregations of the United Methodist Church, Western New York and Missouri Conferences.

Joseph is editor of this series, *Wesleyan Theological Perspectives*, and of the Nazarene Theological Seminary's journal, *The Tower*. He is working on the book of Joshua for the *Cornerstone Biblical Commentary* (Tyndale House) and on Genesis for a commentary series for the Nazarene Publishing House. He enjoys family life with his wife, Charlotte, their two grown children and spouses, and two grandchildren. Reading mystery novels and gardening are other interests.

COLLEEN R. DERR was ordained in 2005 in the Indiana Central District of The Wesleyan Church. She earned a B.S. degree in Christian Elementary Education from United Wesleyan College and the Master of Ministry in Leadership from Indiana Wesleyan University.

Colleen has served in local church children's ministry for over twenty-five years and has taught in both Christian and public elementary schools. She currently serves as Director of Children's Ministries for the Department of Spiritual Formation. She recently completed a series of catechism books for children, entitled *Building Faith Kids,* published by Wesleyan Publishing House. Her passion is to see every child reached with the love of Jesus Christ, and her vision is for every local Wesleyan church to provide quality ministry to all its children.

Colleen is married to Wayne Derr, who serves as Director of Stewardship Services in the Department of Stewardship Ministries of The Wesleyan Church. They have four children, Jerica, Zachary, Tyler, and Anna.

AMANDA DRURY was ordained in the West Michigan District of The Wesleyan Church; she currently serves as Pastor to Students and Their Families at Doylestown United Methodist Church in Doylestown, Pennsylvania. Amanda earned a B.S. degree in Biblical Literature from Indiana Wesleyan University and a Master of Divinity from Princeton Theological Seminary. She has been published in *Theology Today* and *The Journal of Youth Ministry*.

It was at Indiana Wesleyan that Amanda fell in love with and married her best friend, John Drury. They have been married four years and enjoy combining travel and reading whenever possible.

KEITH DRURY is an ordained minister in The Wesleyan Church and teaches pastoral theology (practics) courses at Indiana Wesleyan University. His focus in teaching is on the spiritual formation of the collective body of Christ, the Church. He is a graduate of United Wesleyan College and Princeton Theological Seminary, and served The Wesleyan Church headquarters for more than twenty years in various capacities in youth and Christian education ministries. He is the author of twelve books, mostly focusing on holiness and the personal and corporate spiritual disciplines. Since 1995, Keith has written the weekly Internet *Tuesday Column* for pastors.

An avid backpacker, Keith has hiked the entire Appalachian Trail and the entire Pacific Crest Trail; he also has canoed the length of the Missouri River in a single trip. Keith's wife, Sharon, is a dean at Indiana Wesleyan University; both of their sons are Wesleyan ministers.

J. MICHAEL FULLINGIM is a lifelong member of The Wesleyan Church, due to the faithful witness and testimony of his mother; he was ordained in the Tri-State District in 1973. Mike earned an A.A. degree from Miltonvale Wesleyan College, a B.A. degree in Religion from Southern Nazarene University, an M.A. in Religion from Southern Nazarene University, and both an M.A. in Descriptive Linguistics and a Ph.D. in Linguistics in Humanities from the University of Texas at Arlington.

Mike and his wife, Barbara, served as missionaries among the Wiru-speaking people of the Southern Highlands Province in Papua

New Guinea. In 1994 they established the Missionary Training Institute (MTI) for Global Partners and co-directed MTI for twelve years, facilitating pre-field intercultural training for over two hundred new missionaries serving with Global Partners, Wesleyan Native American Ministries, and World Hope International. Mike also assisted in establishing the EuroCamp ministries of GO-Net in former Eastern Bloc nations.

Mike is a professor in the Division of Religion and Philosophy at Oklahoma Wesleyan University, where he teaches primarily intercultural ministry and related courses. His scholarly interests are in contextualization, oceanic linguistics and ethnography, Islam, and semantic structure analysis of New Testament Greek. Mike enjoys wood-working, hunting, and—believe it or not—tatting.

ROGER MCKENZIE is an ordained minister in The Wesleyan Church and Professor of Religion at Southern Wesleyan University. Roger's B.A. degree is from Anderson University, his M.Div. from Anderson School of Theology, and his Ph.D. from Trinity Evangelical Divinity School. He has served the church as a youth pastor, minister of Christian education, and church-planting pastor. Since joining the SWU faculty in 1998, he has taught primarily in the areas of Christian education and youth ministry. Roger is currently researching the history of youth ministry in The Wesleyan Church.

Roger lives in Liberty, South Carolina, with his wife, Sue; children, Ian and Kelly; and their Labrador retriever, J.J. (Janis Joplin!). In addition to his academic work, Roger is also a graduate of the Richard Petty Driving Experience, Lowe's Motor Speedway, Charlotte, North Carolina.

KEN SCHENCK is Associate Professor of Religion at Indiana Wesleyan University, where he has been a member of the faculty since 1997. He earned a B.A. degree from Southern Wesleyan University, an M.Div. from Asbury Theological Seminary, an M.A. from the University of Kentucky, and a Ph.D. from the University of Durham, England.

Ken was ordained as a minister in The Wesleyan Church in the Florida District in 1991. He is married to Angela; they have three daughters and a son. His recent and current work includes *Understanding the Book of Hebrews* and *A Brief Guide to Philo*, both from Westminster John Knox Press; *Jesus is Lord: An Introduction to the New Testament*, from IWU's Triangle Publishing; and *1 and 2 Corinthians*, from Wesleyan Publishing House. When "deadlines aren't suffocating" him, he likes to jog.

WAYNE SCHMIDT is an ordained minister in The Wesleyan Church and serves as the senior pastor of Kentwood Community Church, a church he helped found in 1979 in greater Grand Rapids, Michigan. He earned his B.A. degree from Indiana Wesleyan University, his M.R.E. from Calvin Theological Seminary, and his D.Min. from Trinity Evangelical Divinity School. He has authored five books, including *Ministry Momentum* and *Power Plays*, both published by Wesleyan Publishing House.

Wayne is married to Jan, and he walks her dog on weekends to win points with her. Together they have three adult children, the youngest of whom joined their family from Korea when she was five. Wayne runs (more like "jogs") about twenty-five miles a week to avoid the occupational hazard of obesity, and enjoys reading within and beyond topics related to professional ministry.

DONAVON W. SHOEMAKER is an urban practitioner living in the New York/New Jersey metropolitan area. Since 1972 he has been pastor of Jersey City First Wesleyan Church, which is a multi-cultural and multi-national congregation. His passion is being an ambassador for Jesus Christ, building bridges of trust and helping to break down the barriers that keep people divided.

Don is a graduate of Indiana Wesleyan University (B.A.) and Asbury Theological Seminary (M.Div.); he was ordained in 1973 in the Penn-Jersey District of The Wesleyan Church. He has served on the Houghton College Board of Trustees, and in various community-based organizations; he also served a stint as an adjunct professor at United Wesleyan College, Allentown, Pennsylvania.

Don is married to Vi, whom he met at Marion College (now Indiana Wesleyan University). They have three grown sons and daughters-in-law, and seven grandchildren. Don's hobbies are tuning pianos and resolving computer problems.

J. MICHAEL WALTERS is Professor of Christian Ministries, and Chair of the Department of Religion and Philosophy, at Houghton College, Houghton, New York. He is also Director of Ministerial Education at Houghton, where he teaches preaching and advises ministerial students. Mike earned a B.A. degree from Circleville Bible College, a B.A. from Houghton College, an M.A.R. from Asbury Theological Seminary, an M.A. from St. Mary's University, and a D.Min. from Trinity Evangelical Divinity School.

Mike is an ordained minister in The Wesleyan Church and spent eighteen years in pastoral ministry, including thirteen years as senior pastor to the Houghton College campus and the community of Houghton, before joining the faculty of Houghton College.

Mike is married to Nancy, and they have two children, Jennifer and Joshua. Mike loves almost all things Australian and is learning to play the didgeridoo.

DONALD D. WOOD is happily hitched to Sally after thirty-nine years of marriage; both Don and Sally have taught at Southern Wesleyan University for the past twenty-eight years.

In 1965, Don earned a B.A. degree in psychology from SWU (then Central Wesleyan College). He earned an M.Div. degree from Columbia Theological Seminary in 1968, and a Th.D. in theology from Fuller Theological Seminary in 1974. He was ordained in 1972 in the North Carolina West District of The Wesleyan Church.

Don and Sally have three children: Andrea, a first-grade teacher in Port St. Lucie, Florida; Micah, an expert car detailer who loves the car club he belongs to; and Luke, who has hiked the entire Appalachian and Pacific Crest Trails, as well as a portion of the Continental Divide Trail. Don enjoys playing golf with his two brothers, Pete and Dan, as well as working Sudoku puzzles (by himself!).